HISTORY

of

RUSSIAN SOCIAL THOUGHT

G. V. Plekhanov

HISTORY

of

RUSSIAN SOCIAL THOUGHT

Translated from the Russian
by
BORIS M. BEKKAR
and others

NEW YORK

Howard Fertig

1967

First Published in English in 1938 as No. 16 of
"Translations into English
of Foreign Social Science Monographs"

HOWARD FERTIG, INC. EDITION 1966

Library of Congress Catalog Card Number: 66-25858

PRINTED IN THE UNITED STATES OF AMERICA
BY NOBLE OFFSET PRINTERS, INC.

TABLE OF CONTENTS

ACKNOWLEDGEMENT

The greater part of this translation is the work of Boris M. Bekkar, former employee of the Works Progress Administration. In view of the fact that Mr. Bekkar was not with this organization during the entire period of translation, Miss Eva Abramovitch and Mr. George Rockwell also contributed to the production.

The cooperation of the Works Progress Administration in every step of the production of this work is acknowledged with gratitude.

CHAPTER I

DIRECT INFLUENCE OF PETER'S REFORM UPON THE DEVELOPMENT

OF RUSSIAN SOCIAL THOUGHT

Peter's reform stimulated relations of the Muscovites
with the people of Western Europe.

This circumstance necessarily introduced new elements of
thinking, at least on the part of those Russians who, whether they
wished or not, helped to introduce the reforms of Peter.

It is the introduction of new elements into the established
order of our ancestors that I term the direct influence of the reform upon the development of Russian social thought.

Europeanization of Russia was, of course, not limited to
this influence alone.

Increased social intercourse with the West gradually
caused a number of rather important changes in the social order of
Russia, and this in turn produced certain changes in social consciousness. These changes in the sphere of consciousness, brought
about by preliminary changes in the external mode of living, I regard as the result of the indirect influence of the same reform.

We shall see that the indirect influence of the reform
made itself felt rather early, although, of course, later than the
direct influence.

We shall become convinced that the direct influence was and could be strong only in the measure in which it was reinforced by a delayed, but incomparably more forceful indirect influence.

1.

When in the good old times, before the reign of Peter the Great, the Muscovites traveled in advanced Western countries, they good-naturedly wondered at the "miracles" of the comparatively rich culture of that period.

Bishop Abraham and Metropolitan Isidor once participated in a church convention at Florence. Bishop Abraham concluded his account of the Palm Sunday celebration in the following manner:

> That was a wonderful "vision" and a very skillful performance in a city by the name of Florence! We describe that "vision" as we saw it, as far as we could understand it with our limited mental powers. A great deal of the spectacle, however, we cannot describe, for it is truly indescribable and indeed miraculous.[1]

The educational level of Muscovite Russia was such that it was actually difficult for its inhabitants to comprehend what they observed in the West during their rare travels. Because of their unpreparedness for serious observation and the study of more advanced countries, those men, bewhiskered and dressed in long coats, concentrated their attention on insignificant details, treating

---

[1] N. S. Tikhonravov, Ancient Russian Literature, vol. 1, p. 276.

important aspects of things indifferently. One can truthfully say that for the trees they did not see the woods. This mental state prevailed not only when fate brought them in contact with the West but at all times. He who, through lack of knowledge, is prevented from understanding the general characteristics of a thing, involuntarily loses himself in details. Here, for example, are a few extracts from The Pilgrimage of the Holy Monk Varsonofy to the Holy City of Jerusalem in 1456:

> The Holy Church of Christ's Resurrection is substantially
> built. In front of the church doors is built a large and
> round annex; the walls are of stone. And on these walls
> are put curved rafters covered with wooden boards and with
> sheets of lead. Thus, the whole cupola is made round and
> resembles the top of an earthenware jar.

Or:

> The Holy Place of the Crucifixion – ten spans long and seven-
> teen spans in circumference, inlaid with diverse marbles:
> purple, black and white.

And again:

> On the way to the Cross of God there are two stairways where
> the saintly Queen Helena found three crosses: two belonging
> to thieves and one to Jesus Christ; the first stairway has
> thirty steps and its width is three sazens.[1]

Monk Varsonofy is so meticulous in his description of various details of the buildings he inspected that his travel notes are considered a valuable source for modern archeologists.[2] But

---

[1]
  Ibid., pp. 284-286.
[2]
  Ibid., pp. 283-284.

this conscientious and painstaking man who measured the lengths of
stairways and the heights of walls says nothing about the general
architectural character of the temples he saw. It is true that he
was not entirely indifferent to their exterior appearance. About
the belfry of the Church of the Resurrection in Jerusalem he says:
"Very, very big and good, too," and that is all. Not stopping to
say anything about the style of the belfry, he hastens to add these
few words about the material of which it is built: "Made of stone
brought from southern lands."[1]

Monk Varsonofy was poorly equipped for his pilgrimage to
the holy places. Equally deficient in mental equipment were the
"Tzar's servants" (or "men of service") who were sent abroad by
Peter to study navigation and other sciences. It would be a mistake, however, to assume that none of them was above the mental
level of Monk Varsonofy; there were exceptions. During the 17th
century Western European concepts began to be assimilated by many
Muscovites... but exceptions do not disprove the rule. And that
general rule was the complete unpreparedness of "Peter's servants"
to judge and understand the kaleidoscopic picture of Western
European social and spiritual life. P. Pekarsky refers to the
diary of P. A. Tolstoy:

[1]
Ibid., p. 289.

In his diary, as well as in all the notes of Russians in
Europe at that time, the first place is given either to a
very detailed or very brief description of what they saw
in their travels. In this way they described cities, villages,
monasteries, churches, various buildings, ornaments, etc.
The reader notices at once that the traveler was interested
mostly in objects related to various church services, religious ceremonies, church decorations, etc. Tolstoy describes with much gusto and with many details all that he
saw in churches, even how the priests and their assistants
were clad, of what fabrics their clothes were made, or what
color they were; how many times the cannons were discharged
on Easter Sunday; the number of Bible readers during the early
mass of liturgy; the number of persons taking part in the
Easter Procession; and finally, the number of candles which
burnt in front of holy images.

According to Pekarsky, Tolstoy even regarded monuments
from this particular point of view:

He was mostly interested in the appearance of the monuments,
not in the event that occasioned their erection.[1]

All of Tolstoy's notes were of the same character as
those of Monk Varsonofy. Yet Tolstoy had some knowledge and was
more or less educated, compared with most of his contemporaries.

The writings of another Muscovite traveler, the unknown
author of the Journal of the Travels of the Tzar Peter the Great,
are even of less value than those of P. A. Tolstoy. This author
does not go beyond the external features of the objects described.
We should not be surprised at this fact. In order to penetrate
further than the surface of things and events, the Muscovites had
first to go through a schooling which their native land did not
possess.

---

[1]
P. Pekarsky, Science and Literature in Russia at the Time of Peter
the Great, vol. 1, p. 146.

The author of the above-mentioned _Journal_, upon his arrival in Rotterdam, jotted down that he saw "the figure of a famous man, cast in brass, holding a brass book, and when the clock struck twelve, this figure's hand turned over one sheet; his name was Erasmus." What did that Muscovite know about the author of _In Praise of Folly_? Probably nothing at all before his arrival in Rotterdam. After having seen the statue in Rotterdam, he learned no more about Erasmus than that he was famous for his erudition. This is not very much! Naturally, then, in talking about Erasmus, he only described the statue. Therefore, it is not strange that after a visit to Cologne he wrote the following lines: "At the market place in Cologne I saw a child with two heads; I also saw there a crocodile of fourteen feet in an apothecary's shop. From Cologne we traveled up the river in boats, drawn by horses on land, etc."[1] This account is not concerned with church matters like the notes of Monk Varsonofy. They are, however, equally as petty; they also show lack of having grasped the main issues.

The Muscovite languor seldom busied itself with generalities. To this should be added that in the epoch of Peter's reforms, Russia did not need general ideas (which were badly needed by France in the 18th century), but rather technical knowledge. This is the kind of knowledge which the Russians going abroad had

---

[1] _Otechestvenniye Zapisky_ (_Notes on the Fatherland_), 1846, bk. 8, "Science and Art," pp. 136-137.

to acquire, both because of historical necessity and the Tzar's

order. Here is an example of instructions given in 1697 to the

scholarship holders going abroad:

> 1. Learn to make and read drawings or maps, and to work with a compass and other navigation instruments.
>
> 2. Learn how to navigate a vessel both in battle and in peace; know all riggings, equipment, and instruments pertinent to a vessel, such as sails and spars, ropes, etc.; on galleys and other crafts, know also the oars, etc.
>
> 3. Whenever possible, look for an opportunity to be on a vessel during a sea battle; those who do not have such an opportunity must learn diligently how to act during such a battle. At any rate, both classes of students must secure certificates from competent naval officials, properly signed and sealed, affirming that the students are qualified and deserving of their commissions.
>
> 4. Those who want to receive preferential treatment upon their return to Russia must also learn how to construct the types of vessels upon which they have undergone their training.[1]

The chief task was the acquisition of certain technical

knowledge. How was this work - then of prime importance - performed

by the tzar's servants? Rather badly.

We must recognize, however, one important factor mitigat-

ing their inefficiency: it is that their "studying" in foreign

countries was frequently tantamount to the infliction of sorrow

and temporary banishment. One of them, for instance, a man of re-

nowned ancestry, wrote home in 1711: "About my life I can tell

you that it is beset with many difficulties and much grief. For

---

[1]
  Pekarsky, op. cit., vol. 1, p. 146.

one thing there is poverty; but the worst is the separation. The
assigned study is the most complicated and difficult imaginable:
even if I put all the days of my life into it, I should not be
able to absorb it. Unfamiliarity with the language precludes my
gaining any knowledge."

Peter had always been thrifty. In sending his men abroad
to study, he did not overload their luggage with money. Moreovor,
his assistants were cunning enough to lessen still further the
pittance allotted by Petor. The opinion of one of Peter's assistants, Feofan Prokopovich, about the bishops' servants has been preserved. Prokopovich used to say that "usually these animals have
predatory instincts, and whenover possible, they scurry and plunder
without shame like Tartars." But, as is well known, the bishops'
servants were not the only animals with a "sweet tooth." Peter's
assistants fully preserved the old Muscovite habit of plundering
the government's monetary reserves, whenever the opportunity presented itself. At times this habit drove to the lowest depths of
poverty those of the tzar's servants who had to study abroad.
Konon Zotov once reported to Secretary Makarov that, when starving,
many Russian midshipmen considered taking servants' jobs. That
was the truly Muscovite method of conquering poverty! Zotov, also
in true Muscovite manner, combatted these "criminal" intentions of
the hungry midshipmen. He wrote: "I have threatened them with
severe punishment."

Moscow knew how to punish and Peter brought that art to perfection. But...who can make merry on an empty stomach?

There was another reason why the Muscovites found it extremely difficult to assimilate technical knowledge. In 1717 the same Zotov wrote to the Tzar himself: "Marshall d'Estrées asked me to call on him. He reproaches me for the shameful behavior of our cadets at Toulon. They fight frequently among themselves and while quarreling use more vulgar language than even the lowest Frenchmen. For this reason they were deprived of their swords." One month later Zotov sent another complaint to Peter: "Cadet Glebov wounded Cadet Baryatinsky with his sword, and for this he was placed under arrest. The Vice-Admiral does not know how to deal with them, for among the French there are no cases like this one. Although Frenchmen do stab each other, they do so only fairly, face to face, namely, in duels. Now our men roam about scot-free." In 1718 a Russian resident in London, F. Veselovsky, reported: "The students of arts and crafts who arrived in the last group have become insubordinate. They do not want to report to the master craftsmen or the supervisors of the works, nor are they willing to sign their time sheets. They demand to be returned to Russia for no reason."[1]

---

[1] S.Soloviev, History of Russia, bk. 4, p. 230.

Under these conditions the Muscovites found the mastery
of even purely technical knowledge extremely difficult. At first,
Vockerodt claimed that these foreign journeys were not fruitful.
He stated that Peter soon became convinced that Muscovites returned
home with almost the same amount of knowledge with which they had
left for foreign countries.[1] Klyuchevsky was inclined to accept
Vockerodt's opinion. He says: "Peter wanted to make of the nobles
educators capable of teaching European military and naval techniques.
It soon became obvious that it was difficult to impart technical
knowledge to the nobles and that a Russian nobleman very seldom became a good engineer or sea captain. Besides, the acquired knowledge
was not always applied at home. In Saardam, Menshikov, together
with Peter, climbed up a ship's rigging and spars and studied how
to make masts, yet in his native country he was a governor-general
very much attached to dry land."[2]

Without doubt, there is a great deal of truth in the foregoing statement. The previous state of Muscovite Russia left after-
effects. In a prior period Krijanić had complained: "Our minds
are dull and our hands clumsy." No wonder that the possessors of
"dull," that is undeveloped, minds and of clumsy hands, had much

[1] I. G. Vockerodt and O. Pleyer, Russland unter Peter dem Grossen,
edited by Dr. E. Hermann, Leipzig, 1872, p. 102.

[2] V. Klyuchevsky, Course of Russian History, pt. 4, p. 314.

difficulty in learning what was grasped with comparative ease by men of advanced Western European countries. Although he contradicted vigorously the disparaging accounts of foreign travelers about the inhabitants of Muscovite Russia, Krijanić admitted that only by the use of force was it possible to induce his people to act and to accomplish something worth-while. He explained this correctly as the consequence of the typical Muscovite's "stern mode of governing." Since the Muscovites were brought to a low spiritual level by these ruthless methods, they proved to be incomparably better prepared for passive opposition and resistance to the reform than for active cooperation. Only with great reluctance did they take part in promoting progress. It is well known that unwilling workers are always very expensive. On the whole, the Muscovites served the cause of progress so badly that the country had to pay extremely high prices for their work.[1] Every socio-political situation has its own logic.

On the other hand, Klyuchevsky's opinion should not be exaggerated. In any case, one must remember that Klyuchevsky himself found it necessary to attenuate his criticism by various reservations. At times he added that the trips abroad made by the

---

[1] How costly the reorganization work was to Muscovite Russia is well shown by the account of P. N. Milyukov in his The Economic System of the Empire of Russia in the First Quarter of the 18th Century and the Reform of Peter the Great, St. Petersburg, 1892.

Muscovites were leaving a certain trace! Compulsory education did not impart a considerable amount of scientific knowledge. Nevertheless it did accustom the nobleman to the process of learning and stimulated a certain appetite for knowledge, for he was learning something, even if not that for which he was sent.[1]

The reader already knows, of course, that under the historical conditions of that time education was understood to consist not in the acquisition of "scientific knowledge" in the full meaning of those words, but merely in the practical assimilation of "technical" information. As far as this specialized information is concerned, however little of it the Muscovites may have absorbed, they nevertheless were able to march as conquerors from Narva to Poltava.

In criticizing the foreign policy of the Empress Anna, Klyuchevsky calls the army left by Peter "excellent." Indeed, this army really was excellent in comparison with the disorganized hordes of service men comprising the military power of former Moscow rulers. To organize the comparatively superior army of Peter implied a certain technical training. In spite of all handicaps, Peter, in addition to the army, created a fleet, "a thing unknown to us before," as Feofan Prokopivich said. One should not think that technical knowledge was then limited to foreigners in the Russian service.

---

[1] V. Klyuchevsky, op. cit., p. 314.

Even in Peter's time some Russians, along with foreigners, displayed considerable technical knowledge. Among them were the following: Alexis Zibin, known as an engineer and seaman; Simon Alaberdiev, well versed in nautics and geodesy; Feodor Samoylov, who studied naval subjects in Holland more or less thoroughly; Leo Izmailov, who served for some time in the Danish army; the famous Vasily N. Tatishchev, possessing considerable knowledge of mineralogy; Menshikov - by the way, not a descendant of the noble class - was not only "territorial governor-general," but a successful military strategist as well. Even some boyars, who, as a class, opposed Peter's reform perhaps more than the other groups of the service classes, showed ability to assimilate foreign "tricks." It is said that Prince M. M. Golitzin the Elder was a good general. The Duke de Liria, the Spanish ambassador, called him a Russian hero, asserting that he was intelligent, brave, well versed in military tactics and well liked by the army. To this eulogy the Spanish ambassador adds that in a less barbaric country Golitzin would have been treated as a truly great man.[1] In one of the following chapters we shall see that closer relations with the West also

---

[1] One must admit that in his own country Golitzin displayed unquestionable greatness, though in a sphere other than the one under discussion. He was one of the very few Russians of high rank who had the courage to refuse to sign the death sentence pronounced on the Emperor's son, Alexis Petrovich. D. A. Korsakov, Accession to the Throne of Empress Anna Ivanovna, Kazan, 1880, p. 40.

altered in part the political views of the tzar's servants, particularly of those of old and noble ancestry. Let us look now at
another side of this matter.

2.

Clumsily, reluctantly, with great labor, with heavy sighs
and vehement lamentations, the old Muscovite indolence was turning
to the West, turning slowly, but nevertheless turning. It is true
that the bulk of the people continued to dislike foreigners, yet
time and again they adopted foreign customs. Europeanization of
Muscovite Russia proceeded without interruption, although very
gradually. During long periods the influence of that process was
confined almost exclusively to the higher servants of the tzar.
This class showed the effects of that influence as early as the
first decades of the 18th century.

The first changes were made in personal appearance, as
happens in similar cases everywhere. Quite early Vockerodt prophe-
sied that the habit of wearing Western European dress and shaving
off beards, adopted by the leading groups of the Russian population,
would not be given up even in case of a reaction. Vockerodt also
declared that the same classes would never readopt the custom of
keeping women in seclusion, or the old-fashioned marriage customs.[1]

---

[1]
 Op. cit., pp. 106-107.

However skeptical the attitude of Vockerodt toward the Europeanization of Russians, he admitted that, because of increased relations with foreigners, persons of higher circles and even many a common bourgeois acquired better manners.[1]

These hints of Vockerodt's are corroborated by references to interesting human documents. Andrey Artamonovich, the son of the famous boyar, Artamon Sergyeev, who happened to be in Paris in 1705, entered the following observations about French customs in his diary: "The French method of bringing up children is praiseworthy. Children are not punished cruelly by parents or teachers, but reared for their welfare. They are induced to cooperate by admonition rather than by the rod."

He was also favorably impressed by the French custom of the free intermingling of the sexes, whereas convention among the higher classes of Muscovite Russia prescribed the seclusion of women. "French women," he says, "in no way feel ashamed to associate with men in all decent affairs, just as the men display sweet manners and courtesy. The ladies of higher families meet daily; they play musical instruments and are not ashamed to sing. Not only Frenchmen of high rank, but even foreigners are admitted to these meetings. They consider the presence of foreigners an honor and a diversion."[2]

---

[1] Ibid., p. 107.

[2] P. Pekarsky, "The Trip of Count Matveev to Paris in 1705," Sovremonnik (Contemporary) 1856, bk. 6.

In his boyhood, A. A. Matveev had received a good education. For this reason it is quite natural that he observed things that escaped the attention of his less refined contemporaries. P. A. Tolstoy, too, upon his arrival in Poland, made similar observations about the custom of association with women. He wrote: "The senators, their wives and unmarried daughters, richly dressed, drive freely through the city and in the country."[1]

Perhaps more than all other influences, association with women, even if it did not change the customs altogether, at least softened the manners of those Russians who had to take part in Peter's reform. Generally speaking, the adoption of pleasant manners began to be considered important. It is known that as early as 1708 Peter ordered lay books to be printed in the now popular type. The first book printed in this type was Geometry and Surveying. This is quite in harmony with the type of knowledge that Russia needed in the epoch of reorganization.[2] But according

---

[1] "Travel Diary of P. A. Tolstoy," Russian Archives, 1888, bk. 1, p. 193.

[2] The sub-heading of the title defines the practical purpose of this book concisely: "The use of the compass and the ruler or the selected principles of the mathematical arts by means of which it is possible to acquire skill in surveying and other related crafts faster and more easily." (Pekarsky, Science and Literature in Russia at the Time of Peter the Great, op. cit., vol. 2, p. 178). In olden times the study of geometry was considered a sin: "Cursed and despised in the sight of God be the person who indulges in the study of geometry," exclaimed the pious men.

to the statement of Klyuchevsky, the second book published in the
"new typography" was not of a technical nature, but one with such
a promising title as <u>Manual of Letter Writing</u>. <u>How Compliments</u>
<u>are Used in German by One Ruler to Another; Congratulations, Con-</u>
<u>dolences, etc.; Correspondence between Relatives and Friends.</u>
<u>Translated into Russian from the German.</u> The publication of this
manual of letter writing shows Peter's zeal to graft European
customs and the amenities of life upon his "slaves." Pekarsky
compares the language of one of the models in this manual with the
epistolary style of the period before Peter:

> In this letter the language is clumsy to the point of being
> ridiculous; every sentence is translated literally. But
> "bowing down to the ground" is not mentioned; no parabolical
> and allegorical comparisions, no eulogies of the addressee
> are used, nor is humiliation of the signer of the letter
> expressed.

P. Pekarsky points out that in addressing a person the
manual recommends the use of "you," rather than the old "thou."
This courtesy formula was not easy to put into practice. Therefore, as the same researcher, P. Pekarsky, points out, mixing the
plural with the singular was quite common both in conversation and
in correspondence until the end of the 18th century.[1]

The specimens of "courteous letters" were translated
from the German. The Germans, in turn, had learned courtesy from
the French, and the French from the Italians. In the 16th century

---

[1] Ibid., p. 182.

Italy was, in this respect, as well as in many others, the leader of fashion for the rest of Western Europe.[1] It could not be otherwise, for in Italy urban culture developed earlier than in the other Western European countries. When Russians found it necessary to adopt courteous demeanor, they could not, of course, feel satisfied with only one manual of letter writing: "L'appétit vient en mangeant." Thus, in 1717, again by order of Peter, a new manual was printed, The True Mirror of Youth or Instructions in Etiquette. This manual taught young Russian noblemen how to walk on the street (without holding eyes and head down); how to look at people (not squintingly or askance, but openly, cheerfully and pleasantly, and with proper poise); how to greet acquaintances when meeting them in the street (lifting the hat at a distance of three steps); how to sit at a table without leaning one's elbows on the table, not licking the fingers nor cleaning the teeth with a knife, etc.; also how to expectorate (not in front of people, but aside). Sociologically, this collection of precepts, The True Mirror, advances interesting reasons in support of these laudable instructions. For example, one must not chew food noisily like a pig and must not speak before swallowing food because peasants do so. The well-bred "youth" must take care, first of all, not to resemble a peasant. Toward the lower

---

[1] Jacob Burckhardt, La Civilisation en Italie au temps de la Renaissence (Translated by M. Schmitt), vol. 2, Paris, 1885, p. 185.

classes, particularly toward servants, The True Mirror shows strong

contempt. It instructs:

> Do not speak more than necessary to your servants or to the
> servants of other men. But if the servants are diligent,
> show them consideration, yet do not always trust them, for,
> being coarse and ignorant, they cannot hold themselves within
> proper bounds and want eventually to become higher than their
> masters. They will divulge secrets to the whole world. For
> this reason take care that no servants are present when you
> want to speak about others. At any rate, do not mention names,
> but use codes or allegories which the servants cannot under-
> stand. These people artfully distort and embellish... Young
> boys should always speak in a foreign language to one another
> in order to get practice, but particularly when they discuss
> personal matters, so that their servants may not understand
> the conversation. Moreover, by the use of foreign languages
> they would distinguish themselves from various numskulls, for
> every merchant praises his own goods and tries to sell them
> in the best possible manner.[1]

In Molière's comedy Les Précieuses Ridicules, Gorgibus

states that the lover acts honorably when he marries the girl he

courted. In answer, his daughter Magdelon exclaims: "Oh! father,

what you've just remarked is worthy of only the lowest bourgeois.

I am ashamed to hear you talk like that; you really ought to learn

how to act in an elegant manner."

In the 17th century a French aristocrat considered him-

self a man of polish when his manners did not resemble those of the

bourgeoisie. The popular affectation of elegance, so much ridiculed

by Molière, was indeed carried to the point of absurdity and there-

fore became a preposterous feature of the aristocracy in its efforts

---

[1] P. Pekarsky, Science and Literature in Russia at the Time of Peter
the Great, op. cit., vol. 2, pp. 382-383.

to be different from the bourgeoisie. Magdelon is not an aristocrat; she is indubitably the daughter of a bourgeois - "bon bourgeois" as Molière calls her father. But she apes the aristocrats,
and, therefore, is ashamed of his display of bourgeois manners.

The aristocratic attitude towards bourgeois manners was
a subjective expression of an objective social relationship, the
privileged status of the aristocracy. In Muscovite Russia the
natural inclination of the privileged to be distinguished from the
unprivileged classes was expressed differently because of the
relative backwardness of social relationships. There the "service
men" thought it shameful to resemble peasant-laborers (and not the
bourgeois, as in France). Pokarsky was of the opinion that The True
Mirror about which we speak now had been translated from the German.
In this connection, it is worth noting that even this translation
does not treat the bourgeois, but only peasants and house servants.
Such an argument was more understandable to the young Russian nobles
than using the bourgeois as an example. Still more comprehensible
for the Russians was the admonition that care should be exercised
in their conversations in the presence of servants, as recommended
by The True Mirror. Khvorostinin bitterly complained of the treachery
of "slaves." The zealous reorganizer, Peter, in his bloody settlements with those "service men" who in one way or another had in-
curred his displeasure, did not overlook denunciations by the "slaves"
of their masters. Since it was not difficult to arouse Peter's

displeasure, sound judgment cautioned the masters to be very careful during their conversations in the presence of servants or to
converse in a foreign language. The tzar's service men were extremely stubborn when they were put to the study of foreign "vocabu-
laries." Bitter to them was the root of learning, but they had to
admit that the fruit of learning was sweet if for no other reason
than the above-mentioned circumstance. There is truth in the
proverb, "à quelque chose malheur est bon."

The True Mirror paid much attention to the topic of
servants. It recommended keeping them under strict discipline and
not forgiving their transgressions more than twice: "He who keeps
good discipline in his household is served well and respectfully,
for the slaves are by nature impolite, stubborn and shameless.
Therefore, it is necessary to break their spirit and to humiliate
them."

Since we do not know the German original - perhaps it is
better to say: originals - from which The True Mirror was translated,
it is impossible to verify the translation. It is certain, however,
that the German text does not use the word Sklaven, but Hausknechte
or Diener. In the Russian translation we find "slaves." This was
in the spirit of our social order at that time.

The trouble with the word "slaves" is that it does not
fit the text. The original instructs masters to discharge servants
who have failed three times in their duties. Many Russian "slaves"

would probably not have objected to this kind of punishment, but masters were not disposed to punish their servants by this method. When their servants ran away from the house, they tried to catch them and bring them back. The following discussion in The True Mirror about the behavior of "slaves" does not entirely correspond to the Russian situation. "One must not," The True Mirror instructs, "tolerate from a servant any back talk or grumbling, for servants always want to have more rights than their masters; for this reason one must not give them any encouragement. There is no greater villain than that poor and proud (but poverty is badly related to pride - G. P.), rascally and repelling servant who is the cause of the saying: 'In the beggar's pride the devil finds his consolation.'" That the servants in the households of "service men" might have been "insolent and scurrilous" is quite possible. But it is entirely improbable that they desired to have "more rights than their masters." Such pretentions are set forth - if at all - by hired servants who have no legal reasons to fear the fists of their masters.

It would be interesting to know whether or not Russian readers of The True Mirror noticed that it is not the Russian servant who is treated in this book. But it is hardly possible to doubt that the methods practiced in Russian households were more in accordance with Russian tradition than with the theory propounded in The True Mirror.

The True Mirror had a huge success. During Peter's reign

three editions of the book appeared.[1]

3.

In this way the leading Russians learned how to behave

properly in society and pay "compliments" to the ladies. Many of

them probably acquired this art with much more gusto than the science

of navigation. The metamorphosis of social habits was reflected

in literature. The heroes of some Russian stories in the first

half of the 17th century use a language that, while preserving much

of the old Muscovite clumsiness, becomes more or less refined and

at times appears affected, pretentious and bombastic. "Falling in

love" is expressed by "being wounded with Cupid's arrow." While

in love, the heroes very soon "become crazy," that is, they lose

their minds. Zotov reported to Peter that at Toulon our midshipmen

were fighting and quarreling among themselves, employing the most

loathsome and despicable curses, for which their swords were taken

away from them. The protagonists in the stories, however, show

themselves better bred men. For instance, "gentleman" Tignanor,

being angry with "gentleman" Alexander, says to him, with a touch

of chivalry: "Now, rascal, you must go and fight with me!" At

every opportune (and even inopportune) moment these well-bred gentle-

men express their tender feelings by singing. Thus, the Russian

nobleman Alexander, being enamored of Eleanor and not expecting

---

[1] Ibid., p. 383.

requital for his love, goes outside the town and, finding there a
"cool place and pleasant air," begins to sing sentimental "serenades."
In her turn, Eleanor, blaming her coldness for making Alexander un-
happy, "cries bitterly and tearfully sings a melody also."[1]

Because of the lack of social activities, the Russian
intelligentsia paid much more attention to the question of sensible
relations between men and women than the men of Western European
countries. This problem was vividly placed before us through the
influence of French thinkers. Even in France, however, the relationship between men and women according to modern ideas was not
established firmly until the 19th century, as in the time under discussion this matter was not taken up even in the West. Russian
"gentlemen," like Alexander, were interested in women mainly because
of their desire to add to their list of amorous adventures. This
nobleman thought of only one thing as soon as he made the acquaintance of either a married woman or a virgin. He flirted freely and
made love shamelessly.

It is not to be expected, however, that the Russian
"cavaliers" of that time, while affecting a sentimental style of
speech, entirely lost their old coarseness. Their ardent love had
an admixture of practical considerations. When the girl, Tirro,
accepts Alexander's invitation to come to his apartment, he meets

---

1
Sipovsky, Russian Novels of the 17th and 18th Centuries, St. Petersburg, 1905, "A Narration About Alexander, a Russian Nobleman,"
pp. 132-133, 155.

her joyfully, and without wasting words says: "I hope to benefit from our acquaintance."[1] Obtaining from her a written admission of love, he is glad "to have a useful letter." Alexander is a gentleman, compared with the other hero of the same novel, the nobleman Vladimir, who in his conduct toward women behaves like the most repulsive animal and profligate villain.[2] Among other things Vladimir passes on to Alexander the sayings of a Danish baron, Foriar, who categorically claims that we all love only for pleasure. But how the Danish Baron understood the word "pleasure" can be seen from the following lines of his song: "Don't give her (the loved one) freedom; do not spoil her; slap her frequently in order that she may feel like a slave and thus fear you." It seems to me that when the author of the novel made his hero speak in this manner, he was describing "poetically" a great many things which he saw at home, rather than the customs of Western Europe, so strong was the custom of regarding women as slaves. It corresponds exactly to the established notions of Muscovites of the good old times.

The characters of these novels developed a taste not only for flirtation and love-making, but also for luxury. Upon his arrival in Zesary (Austria) the Russian seaman, Vasily Koriotsky,[3]

1
  Ibid., p. 151.
2
  Ibid., pp. 166-168.
3
  The hero of "A Narrative about the Russian Seaman Vasily Koriotsky and the Beautiful Princess Iraclia of Florence," in the same edition of Sipovsky.

"rented a splendidly furnished mansion for which he paid fifty gold pieces monthly, then hired fifty men for his household and dressed them in liveries so richly bedecked with galloons that even in the Austrian Court nothing more gorgeous could be found."[1] To acquire taste for luxurious settings was also easier than to study the science of navigation or geodesy.

But let us be just. The above-mentioned novels are re-markable, among other things, for the fact that their heroes are convinced of the supreme necessity of knowledge. For instance, of the sailor, Vasily Koriotsky, it is said that "he became famous be-cause of his training and meritorious service. Seamanship he knew very well; he could sail the seas where islands, and plants, and tornadoes, and winds are found. For this knowledge he was made a sea-captain and was honored as such by all the sailors."

The nobleman Alexander, when coming of age, asked his parents in rather stilted, but characteristic language:

> In all countries the custom prevails of teaching children
> and then sending them to foreign countries so that they may
> learn things to bring them honor, respect and fame. To this
> end, I, your servant, have resolved to ask your permission
> to let me travel and implore your blessings for my voyage.
> I know, my masters, that your fervent parental love will
> rebel against my absence; however, I most respectfully ask
> you to act as parents do in other countries, for by holding
> me you may cause me much harm. Otherwise by what name shall
> I call myself, of what shall I be able to boast and be proud?
> Not only would I have nothing to boast about, but I would not
> even feel justified in calling myself a nobleman! Do me a
> favor, do not let me be forever disgraced.

---

[1]
Ibid., p. 118.

Finally, the author of The Story of Prince Arkhilabon
narrates: "To the German King Friedrich, who was happily married
to Queen Maria, a son was born. He was called Arkhilabon. When
Arkhilabon was five years old he was sent to an academy to study
languages and various foreign instruments, until he reached the
age of sixteen."[1] The action of this third novel obviously takes
place during the middle of the 18th century. It clearly reflects
Peter's opinion of "sciences." Studying sciences, from his point
of view, meant learning various languages and "instruments."
Arkhilabon studied from his fifth to his sixteenth year, and when
he had learned "enough of foreign languages and instruments" he
entered the military service. The latter was again in accordance
with the customs introduced by the reform.

Other sources reveal that the narrative literature correctly reflected the incipient change of views on education. There is
a Father's Testament for a Young Son Sent Abroad for His Education,
published in the first volume of Ivan Pososhkov's works.[2] Obviously,
Pososhkov was not its author, but this is immaterial in our case.
The important thing is the contents of this document. The unknown
author instructs his son in the following manner:

1
  Ibid., pp. 90, 109, 129.
2
  Pososhkov's Works, edited by M. P. Pogodin, Moscow, 1842.

Since, on the way from ignorance to knowledge, difficult obstacles are to be surmounted, I advise you not to waste the precious time of your youthful days in improper affairs or gambling. Remember that there is nothing more valuable than time and its parts, days or hours. When time is lost it will never be regained. It is by the fruitful use of time that all the worthy things on this earth are obtained; moreover, perpetual remembrance and immortality are guided by good deeds and the cultivation of spiritual values. Therefore, spend every day and hour in study and concentration, not reluctantly, but as willingly as possible and with a calm mind.

By stressing the sciences, the father who wrote this testament to his son, showed that he agreed with the conceptions of his time. He writes:

For a practical and rapid method of studying the sciences, I recommend that you study German or, even better, correct French. In the beginning, study arithmetic in the language you will have chosen, for arithmetic is the foundation of and gate to all the mathematical sciences. Then study abridged mathematics, which comprises geometry, architecture and military engineering. Then - geography, topography, nautical cartography and the use of the compass; acquire familiarity with the course of the sun and the principal stars.[1]

Not without interest is the emphasis laid on learning mathematics, architecture, etc. To study them did not imply that one must become an engineer or shipbuilder. These subjects were studied rather in order to enable a native Russian to supervise those foreigners who had been accepted as service men. If the enlisted foreigner, who had been entrusted with some engineering work, should begin "to sabotage his work or otherwise harm the Great

---

[1]
Ibid., vol. 1, pp. 297-298.

Ruler of all our lands, then you, being familiar with those sciences, can detect the mischief, and this will earn praise from your Great Ruler and Monarch, win honor and respect of your countrymen and instill fear into other foreigners bent on malice."[1]

The dislike of foreigners can already be observed in The Discussions of the Valaam Thaumaturgists, and this aversion was bound to grow as more foreigners entered the Russian service. It influenced the future development of our social life and tendencies.

Peter's reform not only taught progressive Russians to respect the sciences and the "instruments," but it also opened a new world to them. The Muscovites have never liked to stay at home much. On the contrary, they readily moved to "new places," in fact, so eagerly that inducements had to be offered to bind them to their abodes. Although at times some "service men" and peasants living near the Lithuanian border looked for places of refuge in the West and emigrated to Lithuanian Russia, they usually preferred to move toward the East. Their mental attitude was also turned toward the East. I recall in this respect how frequently the Muscovite journalist of the 17th century, Peresvetov, referred to Turkey. When the author of The Discussions of the Valaam Thaumaturgists wishes to say: "in other countries," he often makes a characteristic

_____

[1] Ibid., p. 298.

slip of the pen, using an Eastern form: "in other hordes." From
the time of Peter's reforms the whole matter changed. The interest
of progressive Muscovites veered to the West. Our hero, the Russian
seaman, Vasily Koriotsky, was born in "European Russia." After his
travels in Holland, England and France, he "sets the sails" again
and returns to "European Russia." The beautiful Princess Iraclia,
of Florence, telling him of her misadventures and misfortunes,
mentions how "Russian merchants from Europe arrived on ships in
Florence." Thus, Russia is shown to be mainly European.[1]

Vasily also does not lose time in informing the Princess
that he hails from "European Russia." At this point his narrative
gives the impression that our nobleman-seaman felt himself "at home"
in the West and was treated with "respect" by everybody.

"I was sent to study in Holland. A Dutch merchant honored
me by sending me with his goods to France and England, whence I
sailed back with large profits. For this the merchant treated me
like his own son."[2]

The characters of the new novels, written under the direct
influence of Peter's reforms, often do not know much geography and
cruelly mutilate the names of Western European towns and even
countries. But that does not prevent them from confidently assuming

---

[1]
Sipovsky, op. cit., pp. 108, 110, 115.
[2]
Ibid., p. 116.

that all Europe is vitally interested in their exploits. A Russian

"cavalier," having been insulted by an English naval officer, says

to the English king with much assurance: "I hope, and you know it

to be fact, that the whole of Europe will rise in behalf of 'a

gallant and outraged cavalier.'"[1] This statement is, of course,

amusing, but deserves some attention, being characteristic of that

period of transition.

In conclusion, let us comment on two more typical features

of the new personalities depicted in novels.

These gentlemen, diligently studying the art of loving,

are frequently transported into a state of rapture, and still more

frequently sing sentimental serenades. At times, however, they dis-

play great brutality and cruelty. The nobleman-seaman, Koriotsky,

mentioned by me many times, ordered "excruciating pain" to be in-

flicted upon the Florentine admiral who some time before tried to

drown him but who was now at his mercy. "He had the admiral brought

before the tzar's army and skinned alive."[2] This is what Ivan the

Terrible might have done, but, unfortunately, the Great Reorganizer

had a similar temperament.

The "cavaliers" adhered to the old concepts of the rela-

tionship between ruler and ruled. When the Austrian emperor invited

Vasily to sit at his table, the latter replied with reverence: "Please,

---

[1]
Ibid., p. 160. "The gallant and outraged cavalier" was our nobleman
Alexander.

[2]
Ibid., p. 128.

my Master and great Tzar, excuse an undeserving and humble servant.
I am your slave and, therefore, not deserving to sit down with your
Serene Highness; it is proper for me to stand before your Majesty."
Thereupon the ruler replied: "Why do you refuse without good cause?
Since I consider you a worthy person, I honor you sincerely from
the bottom of my heart. Even though one may be my subject and
servant, when I honor him and order him to sit down with me, he obeys
me. And you, a visiting guest...be seated." Seaman Vasily expressed
his respect to the Austrian ruler quite in the old-fashioned Muscovite
way.

When Afanacy Vlas'ev, who was sent to Cracow by the False
Dimitry to represent his tzar in the ceremony of the betrothal with
Marina Mnishek, was invited to the King's table, he refused to eat.
His explanation was that he was a serf and it was not proper for him
to partake of food in the presence of dignitaries. He added that
it was an honor for him to sit with and watch such persons at their
meal; he considered this sufficient reward. Sitting beside the
tzar's future bride during the banquet, he never ceased worrying that
inadvertently he might touch her dress. During the betrothal ceremony, Vlas'ev covered his own hand before taking that of the tzar's
bride-to-be.

Vasily, the brave seaman, resembles Afanacy Vlas'ev in
many ways. In his conversation with the ruler he also refers to himself as his serf, believing this to be required of him as part of

his duty to the crowned head. He did not realize that serf and subject are two different things. We know, however, that although Peter the Great enjoined those who addressed him not to use such self-degrading names as "Van'ka" (little John), "Sen'ka" (little Simeon), all Russians did remain his serfs. The story of Vasily the seaman is typical of the spirit of the period described.

Peter's reforms did not remove the foundations of the Muscovite "Patriarchal Monarchy." On the contrary, this institution was developed and strengthened by those reforms for a long time to come. Consequently, the relation of the service class to the superior civil power not only preserved its old character, but the dependence of this class became even more pronounced. The example of the West, however, did not remain without influence on the minds of the service men in this respect also. Particularly, it affected persons of the highest rank. This showed itself rather clearly a few years after the death of Peter the Great. But about this Western influence we shall speak in later pages.

4.

Pavlov-Silvansky[1] has remarked correctly that Peter and his councillors were far from being without supporters, as was believed by many who based their views upon the words of Pososhkov:

---

[1] Pavlov-Silvansky, Reform Projects according to Notes of Peter's Contemporaries, St. Petersburg, 1897.

"He (the reorganizer), in his up-hill fight, pulls with the strength
of ten men, but millions of men are pulling against him. How is
he expected to succeed?" At present no one would want to dispute
Pavlov-Silvansky's remark. Whoever wishes to question it may be
referred to Pavlov-Silvansky's complete work cited. In this work
the author shows very clearly that many reorganization plans were
borrowed by Peter from his assistants. Indeed, even before Pavlov-
Silvansky, the same idea was expressed and analyzed by Milyukov in
his study mentioned above: The Economic System of the Empire of
Russia in the First Quarter of the 18th Century and the Reform of
Peter the Great. Milyukov asserts that the personal initiative of
the Emperor played a much smaller role in Peter's reforms than is
usually supposed. "Life itself had suggested the topics," he says:
"informed people formulated and shaped them. The Tzar grasped the
principles involved in the suggestions presented by his enlightened
subjects or - possibly this was more often the case - emphasized
the practical side of the matter. The Tzar left discussion of the
details necessary to execute the approved plans to government
officials in collaboration with the originators of the ideas. Then,
a ukase was drafted and promulgated."[1] (The foregoing statement is

1
P. N. Milyukov, op. cit., pp. 587-588.

very important both for the historian and for the sociologist.)[1]
Just the same, it is of interest to know what happened in the
epoch of the reforms after the ukase was proclaimed.

Peter's ukases   always required great sacrifices
from the population[2] and caused discontent. Besides, these orders
abrogated many old customs and affected many deeply rooted prejudices. This increased still more the people's dissatisfaction with
Peter's orders. Even the service class, less antagonistic toward
the reform than other classes, voiced their complaints and opposed
these orders. True enough, this opposition remained passive. The
nobility did not rebel as, for instance, did the Cossacks. But
even passive resistance harmed the cause of reform. Peter and those
of his contemporaries who evolved the reforms or assisted Peter in
developing his plans always constituted a minority. Pososhkov was
not entirely incorrect. There were incomparably more people willing
to pull "down-hill" than "up-hill." Peter, however, wielded his
unlimited power unsparingly and extensively. He crushed the rebels;

1
  Milyukov showed this more convincingly than anybody else.
2
  Pavlov-Silvansky himself said that even the closest assistants of
  Peter did not always support his reforms so energetically as
  Peter himself. After Peter's death the new government preserved
  all his important innovations and transformations, but for the active
  support and further development of many of these innovations the
  government had neither zeal nor energy. (Cf. the article "Inquiry
  into the Reform of Peter the Great by the Supreme Privy Council,"
  in the compilation About the Past, St. Petersburg, 1909, p. 3; see
  also an article by the same author, "The Opinions of Prominent Men
  on   the Reform of Peter the Great," Works, vol. 2, pp. 373-401.)

he met passive opposition with cruel tortures and penal servitude.
His orders were replete with threats. One foreign writer justly
remarked that these orders were written with the whip. But the
emperor and his assistants, in spite of their unwavering faith in
the efficacy of punishment, realized that for the purpose of reorganizing Russia it was not enough to hang rebels, whip opponents
to death or banish the "no-men." They tried to enlist the opinion
of the country in support of their cause. The opponents of the reform did not limit their dissatisfaction to words; they invented a
system of circulating "anonymous letters" and employed other written
protests. Peter did not want to be outwitted by his adversaries in
literary propaganda; therefore, his orders not only threatened barbarous punishment or "loss of life," they also tried to persuade.
From this angle, his ukases represent interesting journalistic en-
deavors.

Perhaps the most interesting ukase is the order of 1702
concerning the call of foreigners to Russia. This order included
a discussion of the purpose and usefulness of the reform. It is
worded as follows:

> In all the lands that by the will of God were entrusted to
> Our rule it is well known that with Our accession to the
> throne all Our efforts and intentions were bent toward one
> aim, namely, to govern this country in such a way that all
> Our subjects, by Our cares for the general welfare, obtain a
> better, happier and more prosperous state. With this end in
> view We have tried to preserve internal order, to protect the
> country from outside attack and to improve and develop
> commerce by all possible means. With the same end in view,

We have caused various necessary changes to be effected in the government to the benefit of Our lands so that Our subjects may more expeditiously study certain sciences now unknown to them and become more skilled in all commercial matters. For this reason We have most graciously proclaimed all the necessary orders, issued instructions and promoted institutions particularly aimed at the furtherance of trade with foreigners; We intend to take such measures in the future also. Since We fear that these matters are not in a state desired by Us and that Our subjects cannot yet enjoy in peace the fruits of Our labors, We have also considered other measures: how to guard Our lands against an enemy's attack; how to preserve the rights and privileges of Our country and how to promote universal peace among Christian peoples. All these measures have been taken in a manner befitting a Christian monarch. In order to attain Our high aims we have particularly endeavored to create the best military establishments as supporting pillars of Our country so that Our army is not only composed of well-trained men but may also keep good order and discipline. However, in order to obtain better results and to induce foreigners who would and could assist Us in the promotion of such aims, as well as other craftsmen useful to Our lands, to come to Us and remain in Our service and Our lands, We have ordered this manifesto to be made public in all Our lands and printed copies of it to be distributed in all European countries.[1]

Here is another example. Promulgating an ukase concerning indivisibility of the estates of the nobles - the so-called "Act of Primogeniture" (the title is really incorrect) - Peter explains the advantages of the provisions contained therein:

If immovable property is always to pass to one son, and movable property to the other sons, the government's income will be more regular, for the master of a large estate has a better chance to remain prosperous while taxing his men lightly. There will be one house, not five; the subjects, instead of being driven to poverty, will be helped because of lower taxes. The second reason is this: families will not degenerate, but will survive sound and compact, and Our famous and great

---

1

Cited in Soloviev, op. cit., bk. 3, p. 1344.

houses will be undivided. The third cause is, the other sons will not be idle, for they will be forced to earn their living by enlisting in Our Service, by teaching or in commerce, etc.; therefore, all their pursuits undertaken for a living will be to the benefit of the State....[1]

Or, let us take the "Religious Statute." This is not merely a code. It is also a work of journalism, at times showing indisputable polemic zeal and talent. In the statute concerning monasteries and monks, in part a supplement to the "Religious Statute," the journalistic element reigns supreme. This ukase comprises a full outline of the history of monasticism, beginning with the ancient Hebrews.

> The Jews had another name for a consecrated person, namely, Nazarite;[2] the ordination conferred only a temporary title, and these Jews took no monastic vow... Christians had created monasticism for good purposes, but later monks began to do "harm to society" and to tempt other religionists.

The authors of the ukase state that the truth is obvious to the wise. "To the rest we shall explain the matter below," they say. And they actually explain it very thoroughly.

Peter looked at monasticism as well as everything else from the state's viewpoint. Did it or did it not benefit the state? He could not discover any advantage to be derived from monasticism, but rather a great deal of damage. Peter refers to that epoch of Byzantine history when the Greek emperors, leaving their responsi-

---

[1]
Ibid., bk. 4, p. 151.
[2]
Numbers 6:18-21.

bilities behind them, "staged performances of choral music" and fell under the spell of "swindlers." These rascals avoided work and fattened upon "the labor of others." They developed their business to such an extent that "along the canal from the Black Sea to Constantinople alone, a distance of about twenty miles," there were up to three hundred monasteries. In other places the monasteries were even more numerous, and all had large incomes. This cancer ate into the vitals of the Byzantine empire. "For this reason and on account of other acts of misgovernment, the Byzantine Empire fell on evil days, so that, when the Turks besieged Constantinople, only six thousand soldiers could be found."

The authors of the decree believed that the monasteries were of no greater benefit to Russia than they had been to the Byzantine Empire: "The present life of the monks is like a corrosive. Although they are restrained by many laws, they cause much harm, for most of them are sluggards. The root of all the evil is their idleness and sloth. We all know how many religious discords and disturbances have originated with them."

It was especially difficult for Peter to tolerate the "sloth" and the superstitions of the monks, because in Russia "almost all of them descended from peasants," and a peasant's first duty is to work, not to debate. When a peasant becomes a monk, he does not relinquish earthly goods; on the contrary, he receives more of them than before.

> At home he was tied to three bonds, his home, his country,
> and his owner, while the monks have everything given to them,
> and, although they work at times, they consider themselves
> free peasants, for they work only one third the time the
> peasants do. Besides, they do not study, nor do they read
> holy books. It is apparent that society has absolutely nothing
> to gain from them; in the language of an old proverb, they
> are "nothing to God, and nothing to the people."

In Peter's time, serfs were not allowed to take monastic

vows, with the exception of those who had a "release" from their

owners. Even in the latter case the instructions were to consider

all circumstances: Who is the applicant? How old is he? For what

purpose has he been released? Does the applicant want to become a

monk, and, if so, why? Can the applicant read? Illiterates were

not accepted as monks.

This order was written by Peter in cooperation with Feofan

Prokopovich.[1] We notice that Peter was not entirely alone in assum-

ing the role of publicist. The ukase of 1714, the so-called ukase

concerning the Right of Primogeniture, cited above, was also based

upon ideas that did not belong exclusively to Peter. Milyukov

proves most convincingly that the ideas were appropriated from one

---

[1] This is fully explained in one of the appendices to the book by
I. A. Chistovich, Feofan Prokopovich and His Time, St. Petersburg,
1868, pp. 709-718.

of Feodor Saltikov's works.[1] Without doubt Feofan Prokopovich was the most active assistant of Peter in the field of journalism. He may be considered the most talented and the most productive propagandist of the reorganization era.

In his sermons Prokopovich consistently defended Peter's reform in all respects. For instance, the inert Muscovite mind did not look with favor on the journeys of Peter and his service men to foreign countries. For this reason Prokopovich found it necessary to propound the value of traveling. In his sermon of October 23, 1717, he says:

> As the river follows its bed, it grows larger by receiving the confluent waters of smaller streams, thus increasing its mightiness and the speed of its current; similarly, travel develops an intelligent man. What does it develop? Physical strength? No, that is weakened by the discomfort of the road. Riches? No, only merchants increase their riches by travel; others lose. What is left? That which founds your well-being and happiness and everybody else's, the finer things of life. In praising Odysseus, the Greek leader, in the beginning of his book, The Odyssey, the famous Hellenic poet, Homer, does not fail to describe him as a man who saw the towns of many peoples and observed their customs. His praise is fleeting, but profound; it is very suggestive, brief as it is.

According to Prokopovich, traveling develops the mind in general and, in particular, the political understanding of the traveler. "Take traveling seriously, for it is the best mode of

---

[1]
"Report on the most valuable statutes selected diligently from government codes of various countries, such as England, Germany and other European countries, in harmony with the spirit of absolute monarchy," op. cit., p. 536.

living and a true political school." Feofan Prokopovich, however,
would not have been the ablest assistant of Peter if he had not
considered the question of the advantages of travel from the military point of view as well. From this standpoint traveling appeared
to him to be most useful:

> How thoroughly traveling instructs in military matters is
> particularly difficult to express...Who could have better
> military qualifications than a well-traveled man, who has
> become acquainted with the countries, the towns, and the
> peoples. Geographical maps are used extensively in military
> operations. But from maps it is not possible to see the
> peculiarities of this or that military fort, its strong or
> weak points, the quality of the training of the troops, or
> the character of this or that people. From maps we cannot
> see what places are favorable or unfavorable for marching,
> fording, camping, fighting a battle, etc. Traveling is like
> drawing a geographical map on the mind so that a man visualizes
> by memory the visited countries as though they were in front
> of his eyes.[1]

5.

One of the most expensive innovations was the building
of the fleet, which also aroused strong discontent. Prokopovich
found it necessary to speak in defense of those ships, in his "Words
of Praise for the Russian Fleet on the Occasion of the Victory by
Russian Galleys over the Swedish Fleet on July 27," delivered in
St. Petersburg on September 8, 1720. On this occasion he emphasized

---

[1] Feofan Prokopovich, Addresses, Speeches, Sermons, etc., St. Petersburg, 1760, vol. 1, pp. 205-208.

the importance of navigation in the history of nations.

To depict navigation as one of the means chosen by God for the purpose of developing the culture of the human race is entirely in accordance with the creed and conceptions of the preacher:

> The Omniscient Creator of the World, considering the need of human friendship, did not make every land of the earth yield all the products necessary to our sustenance, for then the people of one land would consider the other peoples useless human beings from whom no help could be expected. The Creator, therefore, divided earthly goods among various lands in such a way that all countries, being in need of mutual assistance, could easily be brought into one big friendly union. But since it would not be possible for human beings to travel from one end of the earth to the other by land the Omniscient put water between land as a medium of communication. From this we perceive the need and use of a sea-going fleet; therefore, every one opposing the fleet is opposing his own welfare and is not thankful to God for His concern for our well-being.

Prokopovich does not deem it necessary to dwell at length on the general usefulness of the fleet, as it is supposedly apparent to every sensible man. He hurries to examine the particular usefulness of our own, the Russian fleet. What, then, is the advantage of the fleet to Russia? According to his dictum it is foolish not to have a fleet in a country surrounded by many seas: "We are surrounded by water and observe strangers arriving and departing, but we ourselves are incapable of doing so. As a result, our sea proves to be not really ours. Besides, a country without a fleet cannot offer effective resistance to the enemy."

> Just as the dry land animals on the river Nile find it difficult to struggle with crocodiles, so you Russians would find it difficult to meet an enemy along your coasts, if God had not blessed you by sending you a stern warning and had not

aroused in you the ambition to build a fleet.[1]

Thus, the building of the fleet appears to be, after all,
a matter of God's will. It is quite natural, therefore, that Prokopovich
invites his audience to thank God for the construction of the Russian
fleet and for the victory of the sailors.

> Let us praise Him who gave us victory; let us thank Him who
> made us joyful. His work is the Russian fleet, His blessing
> confers power resulting in the achievement of the Russian
> fleet. His volition arrested our Monarch's eyes upon a miser-
> able little boat; He inflamed our Tzar's heart with love and
> understanding for shipbuilding; He predestined the return of
> Russian lands to Russia and the acquisition of new coasts.
> By His blessing, He made Russia strong and powerful on the
> sea, arming her with a fleet, and generously granted her
> numerous victories. Let us praise our God who deigned to be-
> stow these favors upon us! Praised be God's name now and
> forever![2]

It is known that in 1709 Peter asked Prince D. M. Golitzin:
"Does the brotherhood of monks distrust us?" The answer was: "In
all Kiev I have found only one man, namely, the prefect of a monastery,
who is tolerant toward us." The "prefect" was Feofan Prokopovich.
He had been sympathetic toward the reform even before his association
with Peter. It is characteristic that his school tragi-comedy,
Vladimir, the Prince and Ruler of the Slavo-Russian Countries,
Brought from the Darkness of Paganism into the Christian Light by
the Holy Ghost, written in 1705, has for its theme the introduction
of Christianity into Russia. Later N. I. Gnyedich remarked that

---

[1] Ibid., pt. 2, pp. 52-56.

[2] Ibid., p. 59.

thoughts were expressed in this tragi-comedy which at that time it
was even dangerous to whisper. In fact, many considered the tragi-
comedy too daring and damaging to the prestige of the clergy.
After Peter's death, Markel Radischevsky officially complained that
Feofan "abusively refers to orthodox bishops and church dignitaries,
calling them scribes and Pharisees... He calls Russian priests
gluttons, hypocrites and shamans; he calls monks black peasants and
devils. He wants to eradicate monasticism, cloisters and nunneries."
Feofan had to protect himself by stating that he had not criticized
all priests, but only those who are "not worthy of being priests,
not because of their origin, but because of their unfitness."[1]
During Peter's life, Prokopovich did not have to fear complaints,
as the first Russian emperor also disliked "Pharisees"; besides,
Peter could not ignore Prokopovich's sympathy with his reforms.
After Peter's death, the situation changed.

One must not think, however, that in advocating Peter's
reforms Prokopovich was an exception among the priests of that time.
Many priests of Ukranian origin also "tolerated" Peter's reform in
general and the fleet in particular, ex professo, as it were. I
refer to Gabriel Buzhinsky, appointed Chief Hieromonach of the
Fleet in 1719. He preached that a country without a fleet resembles
a bird that tries to fly with only one wing. Furthermore, he con-

---

[1]
See the article, "Vladimir, a tragi-comedy, by Feofan Prokopovich,"
in the Works of N. C. Tikhonravov, vol. 2, p. 152.

sistently stressed the "inexpressible" benefits brought to the

country by merchants. "Not a single country can dispense with

commerce." Another high priest of the fleet exposed the principal

opponents of Peter's reforms, the Sectarians, and translated into

Russian <u>Political Instructions and Documents Compiled in Latin</u>

<u>from Various Historians</u>, by Justus Lipsius.[1]

The custodian of the Patriarch's office, Stephan Yavorsky,

did not approve many of Peter's measures. The heir to the throne,

Alexis, regarded him as his supporter, and not without reason. At

that time, however, the Church was subordinate to the civil power

to such an extent that Yavorsky had to defend willy-nilly "the in-

fallibility of the will of the Monarch." He did so in his own way

and perhaps reluctantly. But he did not let Prokopovich outdo him

in his zealous defense of the fleet; in this he was sincere.

Prokopovich compares Peter with Noah and calls him an

admiral and the first ship-builder. Because of the new Noah, Russia

assumed a much more advantageous position among nations than before.

> Heretofore, Russians did not receive news and information
> from anywhere. They could not study the customs, manners and
> habits of other peoples, and thus suffered abuses, mistreat-
> ment and much mischief from other countries. Russians were
> like ignorant children who are not cognizant of what is happen-
> ing around them except, perhaps, in their own homes.

---

[1]
On Buzhinsky see P. Pekarsky, <u>Science and Literature in Russia</u> at
<u>the Time of Peter the Great</u>, op. cit., vol. 1, pp. 218-219, 492-494.

Now with Peter's key, God opened to Russia the gates
through which she can communicate with the rest of the world. A
fleet is useful not only for the purpose of education, but also
for acquiring riches.

> With the aid of a fleet it is possible to know what is going
> on in the world, to see different countries and to study
> their activities and politics, the beauties of their towns,
> diverse temperaments among men and many novelties. Moreover,
> ships accelerate the rate of accumulation of wealth. This
> one city (St. Petersburg) alone can cover all the debts in-
> curred during the recent War by the income from ships and
> from the use of its harbor. What, after all, do caravans to
> China amount to? An entire caravan can hardly be compared
> with one ship. If a ship is used instead of a caravan, there
> are no horses to be fed or to lose, there are no carts to come
> apart and not many servants are required.[1]

From the start, all these government publicists were convinced that the Russians must be forced to act for their own good.
In his orders Peter continually repeated this view. In his ukase
of 1723 he says:

> Our people are like children who would never begin to study
> the alphabet unless they were forced to by the teacher. At
> first they are annoyed, but when they learn how to read, they
> are thankful. This trait is apparent in all recent matters.
> Everything that has been accomplished has been accomplished
> by force. Expressions of gratitude are heard, however, - a
> sign that the fruits of our labor begin to show.[2]

1
 Cited in P. O. Morozov, Feofan Prokopovich as a Writer, p. 86.
2
 S. Soloviev, op. cit., bk. 4, pp. 782-783.

But one can only force those who are willing to obey. Although Russians were not in the habit of disobeying the supreme power, all government publicists, time and again, stressed the pernicious effects of disobedience. The priests, when pointing to the harm done by disobedience, invariably reinforced their sermons by stating that disrespect for secular authority is prohibited and punished by the supreme power in heaven. There is not a hint of reservations, such as Catholic priests frequently make when discussing obedience to temporal powers.

6.

Western European supporters of the theory of enlightened despotism frequently expressed their conviction that it is necessary to use force. Our Peter is also called an "enlightened despot." This is, of course, correct. In speaking about Peter's enlightened despotism, however, one must not forget the incongruity, stressed by me many times, between the despotism of Eastern countries and the absolutism of Western European countries. The Eastern despot had the right to dispose of the property of his subjects; in the absolute monarchies of Western Europe, the ruler could dispose of the properties of his subjects only in certain cases, established by law or custom. It is superfluous to state that this difference was in no way caused by the higher morality of Western rulers but only by the different interrelations of social forces. Neverthe-

less, the fact remains that Peter, in promoting his reforms, possessed the unlimited power of an Eastern despot, and he used it to
the utmost. Intending to develop the productive forces of Russia,
he began with a complete mobilization of all those available.
During his first journey abroad, Peter hired many foreign mining
engineers. Upon his return to Russia, he proceeded to develop in
earnest the mining industry of European Russia and Siberia. As
early as 1700, therefore, in order to secure the success of his
measures in this respect, he conferred upon everybody the right to
search for ore-bearing lands, regardless of the consent of the landowners. Those landlords who believed that there were mineral deposits on their own land received a prospector's license prior to
anyone else. If they did not avail themselves of this privilege,
he who had the means was free to start to explore, "so that God's
blessing would not have been left underground in vain." Those who
did not disclose ore deposits on their lands or prevented others
from working these were tortured and put to death. Although the
habit of bowing to the arbitrary disposal of their properties by
the supreme authority was deeply ingrained in the Muscovites, they
resisted, passively at least, these new infringements upon their
rights. These infractions were dictated by Peter's eagerness to
develop the mining industry with all possible speed. "Not having
the opportunity to oppose Peter's order openly, the landlords avenged

themselves by hurting the prospectors. Peter discovered that the landlords are abusing the prospectors and are preventing them from exploring for deposits." In 1722 the Mining Department was instructed to inquire into this matter.

Not less characteristic were the measures taken by Peter for developing Russian pearl-fisheries. The ukase of 1715 prohibited interference with the pearl fishing of Captain Veliyashev, upon whom the right of hiring competent pearl fishers was conferred. If men refused to enter his service, he was privileged to force them to work, pay them three roubles a month and supervise them closely, so that they worked assiduously.

As he needed good lumber for building his fleet, Peter turned certain forests into government property. Many forests, especially designated, could not be felled even by their owners. The penalty for felling a tree which was to be used in the construction of a ship was death. Later Peter found it necessary to reduce this punishment. The guilty person was punished by tearing out his nostrils and being condemned to hard labor. At last, even this punishment was found to be too cruel - not without reason, one will agree - and was replaced by a fine: fifteen roubles for felling an oak; for other trees, ten roubles. The prescriptions concerning the extirpation of nostrils and the imposition of hard labor were still left in force for recidivists.

In May, 1722, an order was issued to distribute fine-wooled sheep to those landlords who had more than one estate, in proportion to the number of villages on their estates. Until that time the sheep had been kept upon government breeding farms. The sheep had to be accepted by all estate owners, even if they were unwilling; in other words, the care of the fine-wooled sheep was compulsory. These measures were introduced to develop the wool industry.

In the interests of this industry, closely bound up with the needs of the newly organized army, the landlords received not only the sheep, but also the shepherds. The shepherds were not asked whether they cared to enter the service of the landlords but were drafted exactly as were the pearl fishers of Captain Veliyashev. The working masses of the country were regarded as state property. The learning of trades also became compulsory, and again "for the benefit of the state." In 1712, an order was issued to select the best three hundred and fifteen smiths and carpenters in all districts in order to instruct them in the art of making gun locks, gun butts and gun barrels. In addition, two men in every province had to be taught how to make saddles for the army. All Russians who were skilled in the trades had to work for the state at the first call of the government. In 1709 forty thousand men, not counting masons and bricklayers, were sent from various districts to St. Petersburg for construction work. In 1711 again craftsmen were drafted from the interior for naval construction.

How Peter regarded the working population can be best
seen from the following: in September, 1702, Peter ordered
Sheremetev "to buy agricultural workers selected from the population of the Baltic countries and to settle them in various poorly
developed agricultural regions of Russia that they may teach Russians
how to improve the land." By a stroke of luck this undertaking was
given a favorable turn. Because of the large number of war prisoners,
it became apparent that there was no need to buy Esthonians.
Sheremetev wrote to the tzar: "You have ordered me, Sire, to buy
and send Esthonians and Letts, but your good fortune, Sire, allows
me to send you some of them without having to pay for them. I could
send more than one thousand of them, but it is difficult to ship
such a large number." In spite of   shipping difficulties, however, about six hundred of those war prisoners of both sexes were
sent to Moscow.[1]

While Europeanizing Russia, Peter brought to its logical
conclusion the complete subordination of the people to the government characteristic of Eastern despotism. Not being sentimental in
treating the working population (the "tzar's wards"), the emperor-

---

[1]
See in _Sovremennik_ (Contemporary) (1847, bk. 6) an article: "The
Governmental Economics of the Empire of Russia in the Reign of
Peter the Great," pp. 90-91. Other similar examples were taken
by me from the same source.

reformer did not find it necessary to treat his service men with special consideration (the "Tzar's servants"). The acquisition of various technical information (the study of the science of "navigation" and "instruments") also became one of the numerous obligations of the nobility. We already know that the nobles fulfilled this rather poorly; nevertheless, they did fulfill it to a certain, though insignificant extent. The head of the government, in turn, valued the nobles in proportion to the service they rendered to the state. Peter constantly repeated to the nobility that only through service to their fatherland do they become "noble" and different from the "vulgar people," or the mass.

But if service alone made the noblemen "noble," then it was logical to give titles of nobility to every deserving service man. In fact, that is exactly what Peter did. In accordance with Peter's ukase of January 16, 1721, every enlisted man who was promoted to the rank of junior officer was granted a hereditary title of nobility. In January of the next year, while establishing the famous "Order of Ranks," Peter explained that men of noble birth would not receive any rank until they earned it by performing some service for their fatherland and for the people. A few years before that - in February, 1714 - he had forbidden the giving of commissions to men of "noble origin" who had not previously served as soldiers in the guards and who "did not know the elements of the military profession." In accordance with the military code of 1716, privileged young Russians received commissions only after having served in the guards. For this reason the guards became exclusive. In the "royal guards,"[1] which consisted only of sons of noblemen, "there were about three hundred privates with titles of princes." "The noble guardsman," Klyuchevsky says, "lived, as any private, in the regimental barracks; he received the prescribed soldier's allowance and went through the training of a common soldier."[2] Under these circumstances, a man with an illustrious name was frequently put under the command of one promoted from the very "midst of the vulgar." Thus, descent gave way to rank. This was quite in harmony with that socio-political development which is discernible in Muscovite Russia at least from the time of Ivan the Terrible. The terror-guards of Ivan the Terrible were organized exactly for the purpose of substituting rank for origin. While promoting a policy of Europeanization, Peter utilized to the utmost the theories of absolutism as practiced among Oriental despots. Through some misunderstanding, this side of Peter's reform has been construed as a sign of democracy. As such it is presented, for instance, in some of

---

[1]
Organized in 1719; together with two infantry regiments they were later transformed into horse guards.
[2]
Klyuchevsky, op. cit., pt. 4, pp. 105-106.

Pogodin's historical discussions and in Kukol'nik's "literary" works. In reality, Peter's scheme has nothing to do with democracy. The prominent characteristics of the newly established order are all in direct contrast to a democratic order, because in it all were enslaved except one, while in a democracy all are free, at least, de jure. In the wide gap between these two extremes are all those constitutions which grant freedom to a greater or less number of privileged persons.

The guards became an exclusive regiment of the nobles; Peter thus gave them an organization the like of which they never possessed before. Klyuchevsky remarked that the guards, being a submissive force, a blind weapon in strong hands, became Praetorians or Janizaries in weak hands. Indeed, under Peter's successors the guards frequently assumed the role of Janizaries or Praetorians. But the assumption of these roles did not prevent the guardsmen from remaining landlords and exploiters of the labor of the enslaved peasantry. In the capacity of landlords they made certain claims which even absolute monarchs could not disregard. Compromise with these demands, even to a small extent, gradually destroyed "equality of the unfree," characteristic of the Russian population. Step by step the nobility became a privileged class. Since the organization of the nobility in guard regiments undoubtedly fostered realization of the claims of this class, we may conjecture that Peter's reorganization of the army planted the seeds of the growth of class privileges for service men. Nor should it be forgotten that the nobility which assumed the role of Janizaries or Praetorians under Peter's successors was exactly that nobility which had been constantly urged by the central authorities to keep up contacts with the Western Europeans. It is quite natural then that during the rule of Anna Ivanovna, the Janizaries or Praetorians showed a knowledge of political customs of the West never displayed by the service men before Peter the Great.

The knowledge that noblemen had to acquire in accordance with the tzar's orders was never too wide. From the age of ten to the age of fifteen, the students had to learn how to read and write and study elementary arithmetic, geometry and the Scriptures. After the age of fifteen, obligatory school study was discontinued and compulsory military service began. While, on the one hand, the government took care that service men fulfilled their educational requirements, it took measures, on the other, that education in schools did not interfere with military duties. The order of October 17, 1723, forbade all non-ecclesiastical students to stay in school after the age of fifteen "so that they could not avoid inspection and assignment to regiments on the pretext of study." This order was hardly logical or necessary, for when the choice had to be made

between a compulsory educational program or serving in the army,
the nobles forsook the path of duty with equal zeal. Surely,
schools were not their hiding places from military service.

Sometimes the nobles preferred enrollment in a certain
type of school that appeared to them the easiest, in an effort to
avoid the difficult ones. On one occasion, many noblemen, not
wishing to study in a school of mathematics, registered in the
Zaikonosspask Theological Seminary in Moscow. "Peter ordered the
lovers of theology to be transferred to the St. Petersburg Naval
College, and, as punishment, had them drive piles in the Moika
River."[1]

How could it have been otherwise? Whence could a strong
inclination to study emerge in a social environment previously lacking in any educational facilities? Peter was not the only advocate
of reform in the Russia of his day; it is true enough there were
others, but the severe criticism of the historian may be applied
to many of these "favorites":

> The promoters of Peter's reform were not its sincere advocates.
> They advanced the cause of these reforms much less than the
> reforms advanced them. They supported them out of necessity,
> for the reforms gave them good positions... To serve Peter
> did not necessarily mean to serve Russia. The concept of
> "fatherland" was too high for his servants, too large for the
> stage of their civic development. Peter's so-called adminis-
> trators and promoters of the reforms were in reality nothing
> but his personal house servants... They were true children

[1]
Ibid., p. 104.

of the absolute monarchical government, with its system of
police administration, its army of informers, its contempt for
human life and rights, and with its dulled sense of morality.[1]

Perhaps it would be more correct to say that in the
patriarchical monarchy of Moscow, human life was respected much
less and human rights were despised much more than in the absolute
monarchies of the West. This patriarchical monarchy was unsatisfactory soil for the spread of education. Before Peter's time there
were in Russia a few individuals who sincerely advocated Western
customs and Western science. During and after the time of Peter,
however, such supporters became more and more common. From the
time of Peter's reforms candid eulogists and advocates of Western
culture did not cease to appear in Russia. Russian social tendencies developed precisely in this milieu. One of Peter's closest
assistants, Feofan Prokopovich, mentioned a number of times above,
called this group, to which he also belonged, "the Learned Guard."[2]

The members of that guard are in many respects remarkable
and often even distinguished. It is high time that we become acquainted with a few of them.

---

[1]
Ibid., pp. 333-336.

[2]
In one of his poetical addresses to Antioch Kantemir, Prokopovich
says:
> "And you, since you follow the glorious path
> Of Titans of science, continue to condemn
> The sins of those who hate 'the learned guard'."

CHAPTER II

THE "LEARNED GUARD" AND THE ABSOLUTE MONARCHY

The Russian Occidentalists before Peter's epoch-Khvorostinin, Ordin-Nashchokin, even Kotoshikhin - felt "nauseated" in Moscow; "nausea" is a tormenting feeling. In order to get rid of that feeling, some of them went abroad, while others became monks. These men were *einsame* *Geister* (lonesome souls) in the full sense of the word. They could not even count upon the sympathy of their own class, nor could they dream that the time would come when the government would require Russians to adopt Western customs and the teachings of Western sciences under pain of severe punishment. They had no ground for believing that the Muscovite tzars worked to bring in civilization. Therefore, they did not aspire to serve the tzars at the risk of their lives, nor did they care to come into conflict with their conscience.

They did not deal with political matters; in fact, they did not understand them very well. They did not have the temperament necessary for active support of Moscow's absolute monarchy. In the ukase "Against Khvorostinin" the latter was reproached, among other things, for having used the word "despot" instead of the word "tzar." From the wording of this ukase I notice that its authors did not explain correctly why Khvorostinin used "despot" instead of "tzar." They thought(or at least they wanted to create the im-

pression) that Khvorostinin expressed himself in such a manner
solely because of his misunderstanding of the meaning of the word
"despot." They reproached him only for giving the ruler a lesser
title, but Khvorostinin probably employed the word "despot" in
order to criticize the tzar's unlimited power.

The Panslav, Yury Krijanić, who brought with him to Moscow
the concept he formed in the West that subject is one thing and
serf another, also criticized such unlimited power. Krijanić strongly
disapproved of the "stern government" of Muscovite Russia. We know,
however, that he regarded the wide powers of the Muscovite rulers as the
most potent of all the available means for the reorganization of
Russia. "Oh, Tzar, in your hands you hold the magic wand of Moses,"
he exclaimed, "and with it you can perform great miracles in your
dominions." However, Yury the Serbian did not have the luck to see
the "great miracles" carried out in Muscovite Russia, as he himself
became one of the victims of the "stern government."

Nevertheless, during Peter's time the prophecy of Yury
Krijanić was realized to a certain degree. With the aid of the
"magic wand of Moses" Peter began to perform "great miracles," one
after another. Now, it was not those who were "nauseated" by the
old Muscovite order who were threatened with persecution, but rather
those who were "nauseated" by the introduction of Western European
practices and customs. This means that the situation of our
Occidentalists was completely changed. Now they did not have to

flee abroad or to search for a haven in monasteries: a wide field was opened up in their native country for their conservative activity. Under their eyes Russia was changing her face, assuming a friendly attitude toward that very West whose culture they valued so highly. We know now that the process of reorganizing Russia left untouched - and in some cases even strengthened - the old foundations of the socio-political order of Russia for a considerable time to come. We also know that the Europeanization of Russia was superficial for a long time. But the contemporaries of Peter saw the matter in a totally different light, because at that time no Russian undertook to grapple with basic questions of socio-political life. As to the secondary or subordinate features of social life, both the opponents, as well as the advocates of Peter's reforms, found them so changed that they became unrecognizable. They credited that change entirely to the ruler.

Feofan Prokopovich, the indefatigable supporter of Peter's activities for reform, did not intend to flatter when he spoke of Russia as the statue of Peter and called the first Russian emperor "the author of our numerous joys and comforts, a magician awakening his land from slumber." In his famous Sermon on the Occasion of Peter's Obsequies, there is, of course, too much of rhetoric: the oratory of our clergy could never get along without it before, and, of course, Prokopovich could not dispense with it on such an occasion.

An orator may acquire the habit of abusing the art of rhetoric; Prokopovich does this in his statement that Peter was simultaneously the Samson, the Japheth, and the Solomon of Russia, and, besides, the David and the Constantine of the Russian Church. Furthermore, the art of rhetoric may be perverted by playing with inappropriate words. Here is an example of such play on words: "Peter encountered weak forces in Russia, but left forces of stone, adamant forces to be remembered by." But when the preacher develops such a rhetorical mode of expression, we feel that he revered the grandeur of Peter's work with absolute sincerity.

In Prokopovich's words, Peter, upon his ascension to the throne,

> found fighters that were harmful and malicious at home, weak
> in battle, and held in derision by the enemy; but he created
> an army that became famous everywhere, useful to the country
> and feared by the enemy. In protecting his country he not
> only reconquered lost lands but also increased his possessions
> by new acquisitions. While destroying the attacking enemy,
> he broke down the spirit and the morale of our foes and closed
> the mouths of the envious so that his great fame spread through-
> out the whole world.

His audience could not disagree with Prokopovich - at least those who sympathized with Peter's reforms - even when he defended the epithet, "the Solomon of Russia," which he bestowed upon the dead tzar, with these words:

> Have we not proof abundant? The various "philosophical" arts
> disseminated by his actions and taught to many of his subjects;
> the establishment of various institutions for teaching arts,
> crafts and sciences formerly unknown to us; the introduction
> of ranks, degrees and civil orders; the concept of honest

living, the habit of courteous behavior and pleasing manners;
the metamorphosis in our exterior appearance from awkwardness
to grace - all these achievements prove my point. Now we see
our country incomparably better off than before, both "intrinsi-
cally and extrinsically." We look and wonder.[1]

In order to estimate the force of the first impact of

Peter's reform upon the Russian people, one must remember how the

Muscovites began to look at themselves in the second half of the

17th century.   Comparing the forces of their own country with those

of Western European countries, they declared with bitter sarcasm

that it was useless for the Muscovite "rabble" to hope for victory.

The defeat at Narva showed the truth of the Muscovites' scornful

estimate of their own worth.   But the victory in the battle of

Poltava and other victories before and after it gave them the grati-

fying belief that the time of the "rabble" had passed beyond recall

and that from then on Russia could successfully fight any of the

Western European countries.   Realization of the implications of

this change increased their self-respect and flattered their national

pride.

In his _Eulogy_, delivered on the occasion of the birthday

of the Tzarevich Peter Petrovich, Prokopovich expressed very clearly

the above-described feelings of the Russian Occidentalists of that

time.   Besides, he reminds us that by praising Peter, he did not

mean to degrade Russia.   How had Russia been regarded formerly by

---

[1]
Prokopovich, _Addresses_, _Speeches_, _Sermons_, etc., St. Petersburg,
1760, vol. 2, pp. 129-130.

foreign nations?

> As barbarous by diplomats and politicians; as worthy of contempt by the great and the proud; as ignorant by the learned; as an easy prey by embezzlers; as slothful and worthy of malediction and abuse by everyone. Peter made foreigners respect Russia. Now by his bravery, widsom and justice, by improving and educating the country, Our Most Excellent Monarch benefits not only His Exalted Person, but also all the people. Those who, considering us barbarians, had avoided contact with us, now earnestly seek our friendship; those who damned and abused us before, now praise us; those who threatened, now fear and tremble; and those who held us in contempt, now are not ashamed to serve us.

In his dramatic presentation of the honor shown to Russia by the changed attitude of foreigners, Prokopovich revealed great naiveté. He said: "Many European crowned heads not only willingly make agreements with our Monarch, Peter, but even do not consider it humiliating to shake hands with him."

This naiveté, hardly understandable now, shows that, although Prokopovich was very proud of reorganized Russia - enthusiastically he called her "sunny, beautiful, strong, a loving friend and formidable foe"[1] -, he continued to place Russia considerably lower than the enlightened countries of the West.

In order to rise to the level of the Western countries, Russia had to assimilate their culture completely. Feofan and his friends were convinced they could reach this level through education. But since Peter had started the dissemination of culture in Russia,

---

[1]
Ibid., vol. 1, pp. 114-115.

it was quite natural that they gave all the credit to him, revered
the Tzar-Reorganizer and had the most sincere admiration for him.
Another member of the "Learned Guard," V. N. Tatishchev, stated that
"Peter the Great opened the way to enlightenment for his people by
adopting the best methods of imparting knowledge to them." Tatishchev
wrote about himself in the following manner:

> All that I have, titles, honors, estates and, above all, in-
> telligence, I owe to the grace of His Majesty; for if he had
> not sent me to foreign countries, had not assigned me to re-
> sponsible work and had not encouraged me with his favor, I
> would not have been able to obtain all these things. Although
> an expression of my appreciation would not increase the fame
> of His Majesty and the reverence in which he is held more than
> an added mite would mean to the treasures of the Temple of
> Solomon or two drops of water poured into the sea, I have the
> burning desire to express my appreciation, which is greater
> than all the treasures of Solomon and fuller than the mighty
> river Ob.[1]

Another member of the "Learned Guard," the poet Antioch
Kantemir, also worshipped Peter. In one of his books (Petrida) he
wrote:

> When I mention Peter's name, what do I include in this word?
> Wisdom, bravery in time of evil events, safety, wise precaution,
> love and care, genuine politeness, a justice that is just, a
> builder-tzar, a true friend, a soldier worthy of all the laurels;
> in a word, all that might be called perfect.

Such was the attitude of our Occidentalists toward Peter
in the first half of the 18th century. Later we shall see that
such an attitude among the Occidentalists remained unchanged up to
very recent times. It is important to remember this in order to

---

[1] (No author), Russian History, Moscow, 1768, bk. 1, pt. 1, p. XVI.

66

have a better understanding of the development of Russian social thought. For this reason I shall quote two or three specimens taken from the history of Russian social tendencies in the 19th century.

Byelinsky, in his letter to Kavelin, of November 22, 1847, says: "Peter is my philosophy, my religion, a revelation in all that concerns Russia. He is an example for all those who want to do something useful."[1]

Shortly before his death - as revealed by his letter to P. V. Annenkov of February 15, 1848 - Byelinsky tried to prove to his "trusting friend" (M. A. Bakunin) that "Russia is in need of a new Peter the Great."[2]

In the beginning of his literary career, Chernyshevsky was of the same opinion about Peter I. In the fourth article of his Outlines of the Gogol Period of Russian Literature we find the following significant lines: "For us, Peter is the ideal patriot. His patriotism is of the highest! A burning desire to promote the welfare of his country inspired this great man during all his life."

---

[1]
During the same year, in an article, Outlook upon Russian Literature, Byelinsky expressed the following view on the origin of Russian literature: "Our literature is a result of Peter's reform as are all other beautiful and useful things in modern Russia."
[2]
Byelinsky, Letters, St. Petersburg, 1914, vol. 3, pp. 300-339.

It is possible that the example of Peter was cited by Chernyshevsky in order to mollify the government censors. If there had been no censorship, he might, perhaps, have chosen another example. In reality he wanted to say that the task of the Russian leaders consisted in disseminating knowledge gained by the more advanced peoples, and not in independent exploration and search for such knowledge. In the first place, there was no censorship that would have required him to use such flattering expressions about Peter as we find in the foregoing quotation. Secondly, he obviously linked the task of contemporary educators with Peter's reforms spontaneously and not for the benefit of the censors: "Until we are on the same educational level with the most advanced nations, every one of us has another task (rather than work in the sphere of 'pure' science - G. P.), much nearer to the heart: to assist with all our power in the further development of the work started by Peter the Great."

The worship of Peter spread the opinion among Russian Occidentalists that great reorganizations in our country could be promoted only from the top. This point of view was also shared by Byelinsky. Under such influences he leaned toward the recognition of Slavophile theories concerning the peculiar character of the Russian historical process. We shall see that Byelinsky and his followers could not combine into one harmonious whole such notions and their other social views adopted from the foremost writers of contemporary Europe. These contradictory conceptions confused the socio-political creed of our 19th century educators.

The educators of the first half of the 18th century did not have these problems. The socio-political creed of the "Learned Guard" was much simpler. It contained no elements that could not agree with the conception that in our country everything great comes from higher up. Therefore, they remained entirely true to themselves, not only when they revered and unreservedly exalted the personality of Peter and his activity, but also when they persistently defended the absolute monarchy. Prokopovich, Tatishchev and Kantemir may be considered the first ideologists of absolute monarchy in Russia.

1. FEOFAN PROKOPOVICH[1]

It is natural for Prokopovich, a priest, to have quoted the Bible freely. Referring to the words of the Apostle Peter, he said: "Obey every human being for the sake of God, the tzar as the ruler, or the prince as the tzar's emissary..." He did not forget, of course, the famous words of St. Paul ("the teacher of nations"):

---

[1] Feofan Prokopovich (né Eleazar Prokopovich), 1681-1763. Studied in Kiev; became a Uniat, continued his study in Poland, went to Rome where he entered the College of St. Athanasius. Returned to Russia in 1702, renounced his Uniat affiliations and became a teacher in Kiev Academy. His works include Text-book on the Art of Poetry, Vladimir (a tragi-comedy), Spiritual Regulation. - Translator's Note.

"Let every soul be subject unto the higher powers. For there is
no power but of God; the powers that be are ordained of God."[1]

In order not to leave any doubt about the kind of obedience to the government which the apostle required, Prokopovich
amplified his statement: "Ye must needs be subject, not only for
fear, but also for conscience's sake." Then he calls the attention
of his audience to the vigorous manner in which the Apostle Paul
defended the tzar's authority: "Paul was sent on his mission by
the tzar of Heaven Himself..."

In addition to his quotations from the Scriptures,
Prokopovich also advanced the tenets of natural law in defense of
the tzar's power.

Astonishingly enough, the most prominent publicist of
Peter's epoch refers to natural law first and then to the Bible.
No wonder that orthodox zealots did not regard him as a reliable
theologist. Prokopovich says:

> If we want to understand our own nature, we have to consider,
> besides the Bible, the law put by God into the very nature
> of things. Natural law demands from us that we love and fear
> God, protect our life, "do unto others as ye would that they
> should do unto you," respect our parents, etc. Our conscience
> affirms the existence of this law. To its domain belongs the
> principle of obedience to the supreme civil power. Further-
> more, it is the most important law. On the one hand, it orders
> us to love our neighbors, and "to do unto others as ye would
> that they should do unto you"; on the other, the spiteful nature
> of human beings resists that law. Therefore, one must always

[1] Prokopovich, Addresses, Speeches, Sermons, etc., St. Petersburg,
1760, pt. 1, pp. 249-250.

and everywhere have a guardian, a protector and a strong defender of justice. Such is the power of a monarch.[1]

This is not very illuminating. It is one thing to want
to have a guardian, protector and strong defender of justice, but
another to find that despotism is necessary, passed on as it was by
the Muscovite tzars to the first Emperor of all the Russians and
strengthened by him. Prokopovich says that if people were deprived
of the protection of a guardian and an upholder of justice, they
would very soon cry out that living is baneful without a directing
power. To this answer may be given that powers are unlike; the
usefulness of power does not necessarily imply the superiority of
absolute power. As an intelligent man, Prokopovich was probably
cognizant of the weakness of this argument. He therefore found
it necessary to strengthen it by relating a tale about Veidevut,
"the first Prussian and Zmudian ruler." Harassed by outside enemies
and domestic disorders, the people, not yet under the rule of Veidevut,
asked him for advice. Veidevut said: "You could live very happily
if you were not more foolish than your own bees." The people, of
course, did not understand this reference, and then a sage explained:
"Bees are small dumb insects, yet they have a tzar, and you human
beings have none." Now everything became clear to them, and Veidevut's
idea pleased the people so much that they immediately made him their

---

[1]
Ibid., pp. 245-246.

tzar. This child's tale is not convincing at all. The eloquent preacher, however, is satisfied with the moral of his tale and wastes no more time on it; he hurries back to his original argument and repeats that the whole world shows the need of a guiding power. After this he considers the matter exhausted. "It is obvious that the supreme civil power has its origin in the nature of things." Now our author has only to pass from natural law to theology. The transition from one subject to another is accomplished with the aid of a link: natural law is written in the hearts of men by God, the creator of all matter.

By using illustrations from the history of the Church, Prokopovich points out that Christians felt it their duty to obey even heathen tzars. Consequently, obedience to Christian rulers is still more imperative. The civil subjects of Peter, in the opinion of Prokopovich, are more obedient than the clergy. Thus he finds it necessary to propound the question of the relation of the church to the state.

Some people - according to the words of Prokopovich, they are many - think that priests and monks are not obliged to obey the tzar. Our preacher energetically assails such a notion. He exclaims: "This thorn, or better, this bite, a snake's bite, is the papal spirit."[1]

---

[1] Ibid., p. 257.

Prokopovich states - and this is one of his favorite tenets - that the clergy must not constitute a state within a state. Clergymen have their own functions, similarly to soldiers, civil officials, physicians or craftsmen. Having special duties, the clergy forms a separate department in the state. Nevertheless, like all other departments, it must obey the "supreme civil power." Later this argument is supported by a reference to the Bible: "Having appointed Moses as the leader of Israel, God sends him unto Pharaoh and gives him for assistant Aaron, who is to be ordained a priest. The Levites were always obedient to the Tzar of Israel, and Christ himself pays homage to this civil power."[1]

A majority of the clergy, particularly Great Russians, were against Peter's reforms. Peter and his followers feared that the clergy would incite the people to open rebellion against the movement of reorganization. They did not know yet that our clergy had neither the strength nor the inclination to wage an open war against the civil power. The priests, in their opposition to the reforms, did not go further than an occasional expression of dissatisfaction by some grumbling patriarch in the form of a sermon. Our priests did not and could not have a "papal" approach to the political power, for, in reality, they had for a long time before constituted a separate caste within the state, the class called "the tzar's

---

[1] Ibid., p. 258.

pilgrims." Peter's acts, however, even more than the acts of his predecessors, clearly expressed the tendency of the Russian monarchs to subjugate their "pilgrims." It was natural therefore, that during Peter's rule more of the "long beards" (Peter's own expression) were dissatisfied than ever before. Suitable punishment was quickly dealt out to the malcontents, not only during the reign of the energetic Peter, but also during that of his less zealous successors. The discontented clergy, however, never rebelled openly. Condemnation of every type of opposition by the "long beards" is a characteristic of the "Learned Guard." Prokopovich was not the only "guardsman" expressing this sentiment.

The learning of the "Guard" was essentially different from that of the ecclesiastics. The "long beards" were at best good reciters, that is, they had a certain store of information obtained from reading religious literature. These pious men cannot be accused of having any measure of serious scientific or philosophical education. Men like Prokopovich, Tatishchev and Kantemir, on the other hand, were well educated. It is known that while in Rome Prokopovich studied profane literature, history and philosophy. The Danish traveler, von Gaven, who met Prokopovich a few months before the latter's death, gave the following description of him:

> This excellent man has no equal in knowledge, particularly
> among the Russian priesthood. Besides history, theology and
> philosophy, he has a profound knowledge of and strong liking

for mathematics. He understands various European languages and
speaks two of them although in Russia he does not want to use
any language but Russian. Only in exceptional cases does he
express himself in Latin, which he commands as only an academician could. He is unusually polite and complaisant to all
foreign writers, in fact, to foreigners in general. His death
would put an end to many useful projects.[1]

Another foreigner, Ribeyra, a Catholic monk and, therefore,
rather prejudiced against Prokopovich (who in his books and lectures
more than once criticized the Catholics), says: "If Prokopovich is
to be blamed for anything, then it is for his religious convictions,
provided he has such convictions at all. His library, open to all
scientists, surpasses the Imperial Library and the Library of the
Troitzky Monastery; in its wealth it has no equal in Russia, a country
deficient in books."[2]

Evidently, the Spanish monk Ribeyra was not certain whether
or not Prokopovich had any religious convictions. The Russian clergy
accused Prokopovich of an unpardonable weakness: tolerance of Protes-
tantism. At any rate, there can be no doubt of one thing: the
views of Prokopovich were almost free from the Byzantine influence so
highly valued by the Muscovite reciters. The lay element predominated

---

[1] Quoted in P. O. Morozov, Feofan Prokopovich as a Writer, p. 392.
Compare also Chistovich, Feofan Prokopovich and his Time, St. Petersburg, 1868, pp. 627-628. Morozov corrects the description of
von Gaven by stating that of foreign languages Prokopovich knew
only Italian and Polish.

[2] Morozov, op. cit., p. 393.

in his philosophy so that the dissatisfaction of the "long beards" was aroused.

A story is told about one of the bishops who wanted to complain to Peter about Prokopovich's sinful indulgence in music. According to a bishop's report, Prokopovich found delight in music not only for his own enjoyment, but also by giving musical entertainments to foreign ministers and diplomats. Said Peter to the informer: "Very well, Father, let us go and see whether it is true or not." Upon their arrival at the house of the sinner, they heard the sound of music. From now on, let the story be told by the man who preserved this anecdote.

> The emperor and the bishop entered the house. At this very moment the host happened to be holding a goblet of wine in his hand. Upon seeing the emperor, he signalled to have the music stopped and, raising his hand, he announced in loud voice: "Behold, the bridegroom cometh at midnight; go ye out to meet him. Happy is the worthy servant, and grief is the lot of the unworthy! Be well, Most Gracious Master!" At this time all the guests received goblets filled with wine and all drank to the health of His Majesty. The emperor, turning to the bishop, said: "If you so desire, you may remain here, but if you do not care to stay, you have my permission to leave. I shall remain in such pleasant company."[1]

The bishop-informer probably felt very miserable when he returned home, leaving Peter in the "pleasant company" of Feofan Prokopovich and his foreign guests. Feofan Prokopovich was promoted

---

[1] I. I. Golikov, Deeds of Peter the Great, vol. 15, p. 212; quoted by Chistovich, op. cit., pp. 628-629.

to high posts: first he was bishop of Pskov, then of Novgorod.
In view of his education and his habits, he undoubtedly felt ill
at ease in an ecclesiastical environment. This dislike alone was
to him a powerful motive for siding with Peter in the latter's
struggle with the recalcitrant clergy.

In the outlook of the other members of the "Learned Guard"
the "lay element" was even more developed than in Prokopovich. As
we shall soon see, Tatishchev was strongly prejudiced against the
priesthood; by some of them he was suspected of "atheism." Even
Prokopovich, who maintained friendly relations with Tatishchev, was
frequently embarrassed by his mocking and sarcastic remarks about
some biblical passages.[1] Obviously, in view of such an attitude
toward the clergy, the "Learned Guard" was reluctant to recognize
Tatishchev's high and important official position.

Why, with all his education, Prokopovich could advance
only flimsy arguments in behalf of absolute monarchy is not very
clear. Without quoting again his Sermon on the Tzar's Power and
Honor and his other sermons, I shall cite here another of his arguments in support of absolutism. This argument really contains the
essence of all the others. It was expressed by Prokopovich after

---

[1]
One of the disputes with Tatishchev suggested to Prokopovich his
essay, "About the Book of Solomon Called the Song of Songs."
(Chistovich, op. cit., pp. 613-614.)

Peter's death; its meaning can be reduced to the following: "Monarchy is the only natural system of government for Russia; any other system will only bring disorder and misery to the Russian people."[1]

This viewpoint was as unsound as were the arguments in defense of despotism offered by the Muscovites of the early 17th century in their disputes with Maskiewicz, a Polish savant. Nevertheless, it is instructive just because of its utter lack of theoretical substance. This shows that not Western science, but pungent reality induced Prokopovich to defend absolutism. Plain facts convinced the "Learned Guard" that the strong ruling hand of a tzar favoring the education of the people would be the surest support of their own educational aspirations. The "Learned Guardsmen" were not interested in wrenching away the "magic wand of Moses" from the tzar's hand.

It is understood that their eagerness for education was not the only thing considered by the "Learned Guard." During the reign of Peter I, "birth" gave way to "the system of ranks." In the reign of Peter II, "birth" made an effort to regain some of its privileges lost during the reign of Peter I. The situation of the "Learned Guard" then became very difficult. The melancholy poetical

---

[1] This argument was expressed by Prokopovich in his description of the "little schemes" of the close councillors of Peter.... It was printed in the addendum to the translation of Notes of the Duke de Liria and Borwick by D. Yazikov, St. Petersburg, 1845. The above mentioned thesis can be found on page 199.

work of Prokopovich, "The Little Shepherd Cries During the Many
Rainy Days," relates to that time and expresses the mood of our
educators quite well. Prokopovich complains:

> How long will I have to wait for the gracious favor of the
> clear skies? Nowhere can I see a bit of blue sky. I see
> nothing but rain. Hope is no more, only gloom and unhappi-
> ness. But then a silver lining appears in the clouds - it
> tantalizes. The herd again begins to have faith, something
> is shining, but it is deceptive.

In such a situation there was but one hope, that another
tzar, capable of using the "wand of Moses" properly, would come
forth. It is clear, therefore, that Prokopovich and his cobelievers
had to oppose with all their might any attempt to shorten the power
of the magic instrument.

Even the French educators of the second half of the 18th
century - men brought up in an historical environment far different
from the Russian - placed much hope in the "wand of Moses." The
belief in enlightened despotism was strong and widespread throughout the century. Voltaire was able to pay magnificent compliments
to the "ruler-philosophers." Even Diderot, a born enemy of sover-
eigns, uttered such compliments.

We already know that Russian absolutism was very different from that of Western Europe. Peter's reform not only left in-
tact the peculiar features of the Russian socio-political order,
but, in fact, brought them into bold relief. For this reason the

Russian apostles of enlightened despotism were obliged to accept
methods of government that had nothing to do with enlightenment.
The expression, "We are new men in everything," belongs to Peter.
Despite this, he retained a great deal of the old order in his
governmental setup and what an order it was! When the cruel
Romodanovsky - according to his own words - was swimming in blood,
in the Preobrajensky village, it was quite in the spirit of Peter's
rule. Prokopovich knew of the tzar's cruel methods in dispatching
his opponents; nevertheless, he "administered him full absolution,"
as has been excellently stated by Morozov. The Russian believers
in the magic of "Moses' wand" had to reconcile themselves to much
more than these bloody settlements. These punishments were preceded
by denunciations, and new accusations developed during tortures.
Since every situation has a logic of its own, the leader of the
"Learned Guard" had to play the informer, and this information was
then analyzed in a torture chamber. In his struggle with the old
church party, particularly in the dark epoch of Biron, our "little
shepherd" (Prokopovich) showed that he was not only a sly fox with
a soft bushy tail, but also a big bad wolf with very sharp teeth.
"Priests and monks were crushed like flies and executed or deprived
of their titles," says a later preacher, recollecting events of that
epoch. "Endless streams of men were taken by land and by water.
Whither? For what purpose? Priests, monks, and pious men were
taken to Okhotsk, to Kamchatka, to Orenburg... Those were bad times."

80

Morozov, from whose work I quote the words of this preacher, adds

to this: "The archinstigator of those dreadful times was Feofan."[1]

He recognizes Prokopovich as a leader, but only in ecclesiastic

matters. If one wants to understand the character of the leader of

the "Learned Guard," it is enough to restrict the study to this field

of denunciations and ruthless tortures.

Of course, although the "pious men" suffered a great deal

from the enlightened "little shepherd," they did not have anything

against denunciations or the torture-chamber as such, provided they

could use them for their own purposes. Not only did they not oppose

these denunciations, but they actually resorted to them in their

feud with Prokopovich. The "pious men," in their turn, made Prokopovich

go through many anxious and uneasy hours. These men, however, had

always clung to stagnation, while Prokopovich, with all the "Learned

Guard," aspired to progress and enlightenment.

Morozov explained that the odious acts of Prokopovich were

dictated to him by the strict logic of his social status:

> Recognizing that the further development of Russia was possible
> only in the direction of Peter's policy, to which he had lent
> his whole-hearted support, Prokopovich proved himself beyond
> doubt an active supporter of the government, even though it
> was headed by Biron. In all the discussions of this period
> one sees the development of the syllogism: Peter's projects
> had as their aim the people's welfare; at the present time
> these projects are encouraged by the government; consequently,
> Russia is thriving and prospering; the oppositionists are

---

[1] G. P. Morozov, op. cit., p. 357.

"sinister gossip-mongers" and traitors; they should therefore be destroyed. The role of official spokesman undertaken
by Prokopovich (a role which he did not abandon until the end
of his life) naturally prevented him from adopting any other
form of reasoning. It should be recalled that in the heyday
of his activity nothing could be published or promulgated
without the tzar's approval and then only through official
channels; this "exchange of opinions" took place through the
pages of Preobrajensky's <u>Prikaz</u>. This is enough to understand
why Prokopovich could not reason differently.[1]

Now I shall ask the reader to concentrate on a part of a
sermon delivered in 1708 by Stephan Yavorsky, an opponent of
Prokopovich.... In it Yavorsky showed himself also a defender of
Peter's reforms. It is interesting to note here that, although he
disapproved of many of Peter's acts, Yavorsky, in his usual vivid
and insistent manner, warned Russia against harboring any idea of
resisting the tzar's rule. He appealed to his fellow-countrymen
in these words:

> Load the ships with all kinds of goods and trade in all
> countries; buy, sell, prosper; only look out, for Heaven's
> sake, for the creeping snakes, the mutineers, who, like the
> serpent of paradise, whisper malice into the ears of the care-
> less: "You will not die but will become like gods; have only
> a will to power." Be careful of such venomous snakes and
> scorpions; do not trust them. A lie is a lie. The seducing
> serpents shall perish, and with them the seduced... If you
> lend them your ears, I assure you that they will cause you
> much grief. The worst calamities are visited upon you not
> by foreign enemies, but by those within our land.[2]

---

[1] <u>Ibid</u>., p. 360.

[2] <u>Ibid</u>., pp. 86- 87.

Both in form and content this passage may be compared with Prokopovich's condemnation of the opponents of the tzar's rule, of Peter's critics and the "sinister gossip-mongers." This means that, in a political sense, our leader of the "Learned Guard" did not go beyond the viewpoint expressed by his implacable adversary Yavorsky, who was inclined to be conservative and approved only with many reservations the reforms of Peter.

There are other considerations. Our educated Westerner did not go further than Ivan Peresvetov, who also was a conscientious supporter of absolute monarchy of the Oriental type. But Peresvetov brought to the fore the question of freeing the enslaved serfs. He used to say that in the Byzantine Empire, at the time of Constantine, the best people were sold as slaves. For this reason the army lacked courage to fight and ran away from the battlefield. When these captives were freed they became warriors. Prokopovich was never disturbed by such sociological phenomena.

The status of the people, who paid a very dear price for the reorganization of Russia, apparently concerned Prokopovich less than it interested some of his contemporary visionaries or members of the Supreme Secret Council. They were disturbed by the extreme poverty of the peasantry, if only for the reason that "where there are no peasants, there are no soldiers."

2. VASILY NIKITICH TATISHCHEV[1]

Despite their friendly relations, Prokopovich was greatly irritated by Tatishchev's harsh and bold criticism of "The Song of Songs."[2] Prokopovich attacked the "wise fools who speak so disrespectfully about this biblical story." This is offensive enough, but as an appraisal of Vasily Nikitich Tatishchev it is entirely unjust; it is possible that he was not versed in theology, but in other things he was far from being a "wise fool." He was noted for his "logical reasoning," which was his strength as well as his weakness. Apart from this he was, like Prokopovich, one of the best educated Russians of the time. His library included the works of Machiavelli, Newton, Descartes, Hobbes, Locke's treatise "Of Civil Government," and others.[3] He was acquainted with the works of Bayle. In Russian history and geography, as well as in the history of Russian jurisprudence, he was an original thinker. He was well versed

---

[1]
Tatishchev, V. N., 1686-1756, of noble birth; staunch supporter of Peter's Reform, a distinguished enlightener, statesman and historian. Major works: History of Russia since Ancient Times; Utilitarianism and Natural Law; Spiritual Testament and Instruction to my son Ergraf. - Translator's note.

[2]
Tatishchev claimed that Solomon in writing the book was inspired by a passionate love for his bride, an Egyptian princess, and therefore the subject matter treated was nothing but pure sex.

[3]
N. Popov, Tatishchev and His Time, St. Petersburg, 1861, p. 433.

in the political and philosophical literature of that time.[1]

Precisely because he was not a theologian, his opinions, in comparison with those of Prokopovich, had the important advantage of being free from scholastic chaff and being entirely worldly. This phase of his views makes him one of the most interesting representatives of that Russian type which was molded under the direct influence of Peter's reforms.

In Muscovite Russia, education had an "ecclesiastical" character; with very few exceptions it was monopolized by the priests, who, moreover, studied rarely and reluctantly. Peter's reforms, in one way or another, opened education to a new class and forced it to study the applied sciences in preference to metaphysics. The new studies created in the better minds of this class the strong conviction that learning should be comprehensive, diligent and continuous. The "Learned Guard" defended this conviction with much zeal, stressing secular knowledge above all. All the supporters of the reforms agreed on this point. Even Saltikov had advised Peter to substitute books of "universal and lay histories" for theological works in teaching reading and writing; he urged that books

---

[1]
Tatishchev says about himself, that he "is not educated in philosophy." This undoubtedly is unnecessary modesty. Perhaps of all the philosophers, Christian Wolf was held by him in the highest esteem. He was a follower of Wolf in all that related to the "origin of communities, orders, governments and the respective duties of rulers and subjects." He disagreed with the political teachings of Machiavelli, Locke and Hobbes.

for this purpose be translated into Russian.[1]

In his Discussion of Two Friends Concerning the Usefulness of Education and the Sciences, written in 1733 and later re-
vised, Tatishchev assumes that "intelligence in children is true
joy," but that in order to become intelligent the child must first
study. We find in the Discussion a complete and variegated program
for those sciences the acquisition of which Tatishchev recommends
most persistently. Although, as "Peter's nestling," Tatishchev re-
gards science almost exclusively from the utilitarian point of view,[2]
his program, if only because of its wide scope, suggests how great
was the gap separating the educated men of Peter's time and the reciters of Muscovite Russia. This program is the more remarkable because it clearly reveals his lay outlook on education. The example

---

[1] Pavlov-Silvansky, Reform Projects according to Notes of Peter's
Contemporaries, St. Petersburg, 1897, p. 24.

[2] "Why must one study geography? The description of land or geography
shows not only the relative location of places - which might be
useful in times of warfare, in that it helps to acquaint a person
with the difficulties and possibilities of fortification and army
movements in that country - but also the character of the people,
the climatic condition of the country, its products and resources
and the things which it lacks. First we must know our own country,
then the adjacent countries with which we have business transactions,
or from which we may expect possible assistance in case of necessity,
or even an attack. Those countries must be known well in order
that one may sensibly discuss various government affairs and orders,
and not act as a blind man who speaks of colors, etc." Tatishchev,
Discussions of the Usefulness of the Sciences and of Schooling,
with introduction by N. Popov, Moscow, 1887, pp. 81-82.

of Tatishchev indicates that Peter's reforms terminated the predominance of the theological element in the philosophy of educated
Russians.

It is worth noting that, in general, Tatishchev was not
favorably disposed toward the clergy. He considered the influence
of this class upon social progress more harmful than useful. He
claimed, for instance, that in Russia, as early as the coming of
Christianity, there were many schools in which even Greek and Latin
were studied. The yoke of the Tartars, while weakening the power
of the tzars, increased the importance of the priesthood, and the
latter "stopped all teaching in the schools and churches and devoted all their energies to increasing their power, their estates
and income, at the expense of the people, whom they kept in ignorance
and superstition."[1] In another place, answering those critics who
hold that science undermines religion, he says that such statements
could be made only by "the ignorant,   uninstructed in the true
principles of philosophy," or by "some villainous church officials"
who, in the interest of their class, wish "to keep the people in
the dark and to prevent them from understanding any truth, and would
have them submit blindly and slavishly to their word and command."[2]

---

[1]
N. Popov, op. cit., p. 514.
[2]
Tatishchev, op. cit., p. 58.

At this point Tatishchev adds - perhaps because of considerations
for his own safety - that the strongest opponents of education were
the Roman Catholic priests: "Rome's archbishops showed themselves
to be more opposed to it than all the others. They spent much
effort to keep the people in darkness and superstition."[1]

This criticism of the priesthood deserves special attention. At an earlier period of its history Muscovite Russia knew
the antagonism between the service men on one side and the clergy
on the other. For the source of this discord we must look to the
controversy about land, which was the most important economic issue
and, therefore, the most exciting political question in the Muscovite Russia of that time. The clergy tried to keep and increase
their landed estates. The service men, on the contrary, were
interested in transferring these landed estates to the dominions
of the tzar, who was in the habit of allotting such estates to his
"servants" as rewards. This antagonism was transmitted to the
Russia of Peter's time. It can easily be seen in the willingness
of the service men of that time to support all government measures
designed to curtail the political influence and, above all, the
property rights of the Church. Its most ardent enemies were "Peter's
nestlings."

1
 Ibid., p. 58.

Our author was particularly interested in utilizing the incomes of the monasteries. He praised greatly Peter's ukases which compelled the monasteries in all the districts, provinces and towns to open schools and maintain them at their own expense. He thought that monasteries had superfluous incomes, "over and above the funds necessary for the maintenance of the churches. There are enough of these incomes to maintain schools, and God will be pleased that such uselessly hoarded money is to be employed for something useful in His name and for the benefit of the whole country."[1]

Ivan III had already been toying with the idea that God would be pleased if the lands in the hands of the monks passed into the possession of the tzar. He was unable, however, to realize this pious idea. In his reign the government was obliged to enter into a bargain with the clergy. Temporarily the government gave up the idea of expropriating the ecclesiastical estates, rewarding itself generously for this concession by a methodical and progressive interference in the financial affairs of the churches. Under Peter and his successors this intervention of the central government became a matter of serious concern to the Church. During Peter's reign, however, the climax could not be foreseen. Although Peter was not opposed to measures that would compel the clergy to

---

[1]
Ibid., p. 154. Compare also p. 243, comments upon the second book of "Russian History," p. 425.

relinquish their land "in the name of God," such course of action

could not be taken until the reign of Catherine II. The priesthood

was too useful an instrument to the central power to have its

interests ignored entirely, even by such a despot as Peter. Nor

did the nobility wish a complete rupture with the priests. Only

the revolutionary bourgeoisie of France contrived to effect a com-

plete break with the Church, and that only for a very short time.

Therefore even the representatives of the educated Russian aris-

tocracy who had the least friendly feelings toward the clergy ad-

hered to their traditional policy and went no further than to adopt

the Protestant policy as to the relation between Church and State.

This point of view we find also in Tatishchev.

Tatishchev fully recognizes the "incontrovertible state-

ments of the Holy Scriptures." He does not doubt at all that man

is composed of two "elements," body and soul. Referring to the

teaching about the nature of the soul, he proves its immortality:

"The essence of the soul is the spirit, destitute of matter and of

component parts; consequently the soul is indestructible, and, there-

fore, immortal."[1] (Radishchev also resorted to the same argument in

his attempt to justify the radical deductions of the liberal French

philosophy of the 18th century.) Down to the very end of the 18th

_____

[1]
Ibid., p. 7.

century this argument was considered irrefutable by all thinkers
who were prone to compromise with the theologians, and such thinkers
were in the majority, particularly in Germany.

I should not like to define at this point the theoretical
value of this argument. In order to characterize properly Tatishchev'
philosophy, it is important to note that his idea of the two "elements" or properties of man serves as his basis for classifying the
sciences. He says: "The sciences are divided by philosophers into
two classes: philosophy (natural science) and theology (spiritual
science)."[1] Thus, "theology" has its own field of study. Tatishchev
carefully avoids encroaching upon its domain. On the contrary, he
tries sedulously to guard the "physical" field of "philosophy" from
theological interpretations. Even the principles of morality are
based, in his opinion, not upon religious commandments, but upon
"natural law, which was inculcated upon our hearts at the time of
the creation of Adam."[2] Natural law "in everything, particularly
in the most important matters," is in perfect agreement with the
"written" law declared by God through his prophets and later re-
asserted and interpreted by Jesus Christ.[3] In order to prove this,

---

[1]
Ibid., p. 76.
[2]
Ibid., p. 20.
[3]
Ibid., p. 20-21.

Tatishchev compares the principle of the "written" law with the principle of natural law. "The basis of the latter - to love oneself sensibly - tallies with the foundation of the written law," he says, "because sensible love of oneself is the mainspring of all virtues; but excessive love of oneself or selfishness is the causes of all evil."[1] In his effort to found all the principles of morality upon a moderate love of oneself, Tatishchev appears to us as a typical "enlightener" of the 18th century - as an _Aufklärer_, as the Germans say. In this respect, however, the educators of the 18th century were not different from the educators of other epochs. Socrates, as he was depicted by Xenophon, also founded morality upon sensible egoism. Chernyshevsky, Dobrolyubov, Pisarev - our educators of the 1860's - did the same.

According to Tatishchev, we must love God because of sensible egotistical considerations. "Although I am the most insignificant thing in the world," he says, "I must declare that I am created by Him, and that whatever I have, I have because of Him; ergo, I must love Him as my father and benefactor. Besides, as I always wish to increase my well-being, and know that I cannot get it from anybody except Him, I must _a priori_ glorify God."[2] This

---

[1]
Ibid., p. 22.
[2]
Ibid., p. 22.

is almost laughable. Only sociology can give us a true basis for principles of morality. The enlighteners were hardly capable of clarifying the problem of human relationships. Let us not reproach Tatishchev because he was not a sociologist; let us rather turn our attention to the strong side of his views.

Trying to defend the domain of "natural" philosophy from theological encroachments, he becomes sincerely indignant at having to put up a defense against the vituperations heaped upon men of science and ideas by religious fanatics. Socrates, "slandered as an atheist and evil-doer and sentenced to death, was later acknowledged as the wisest man in all Greece; he was praised by Christian and heathen alike...and there was no doubt about his salvation."[1] Tatishchev was vexed still more by accusations that came from Christians. "It is particularly sad to see," he writes, "that highly intelligent men are slandered without reason..."[2]

Tatishchev advocated religious tolerance. He sternly criticized the persecution of Sectarians, although he regarded them as "crazy." True to his utilitarian principles, he points out that religious struggles bring much harm to the government and emphasizes that they are brought about by avaricious priests and superstitious

---

[1] Ibid., p. 48.
[2] Ibid., p. 49.

hypocrites. "Among intelligent men such persecutions and strifes cannot occur, because to the wise it does not matter whether the man who lives with him in the same city is Lutheran, Calvinist or heathen; likewise, when he trades, he does not consider the creed of the man but his goods, his actions and his behavior."[1] This is almost worthy of Voltaire! It is not surprising, however, Tatishchev had not read in vain the works of Pierre Bayle, the wise, persistent prophet of tolerance. As is well known, Bayle propounded the theory that a country not only cannot be harmed by a difference of religious views among the people, but that, on the contrary, such divergence is likely to benefit it and that society could even exist with no religion whatsoever (the society of atheists). With this last statement Tatishchev, perhaps, would not agree. In his last will and testament he appears to us as a faithful Christian who also followed Bayle in avoiding any prejudices against atheists. We have seen that Tatishchev did not consider unity of religious belief necessary.

In the days of Tatishchev the greatest task of humanity was to realize that ethics is independent of religion.[2] Tatishchev understood this very well, and in this connection we like to make

---

[1] Ibid., p. 71.

[2] Compare Ludwig Feuerbach's Complete Works, vol. 5 (Pierre Bayle), Stuttgart, 1905, p. 193. See also Ibid., p. 319: "Bayle's importance for philosophy lies principally... in his negative relation to theology."

the following comment:

> From the study of the <u>Discussions</u> it may be seen that the
> "prejudiced Pharisees" are not the only ones who slander the ad-
> vocates of new teachings. "Epicurus, who lived 450 years before
> Christ," we are told, "was maliciously accused by many and was called
> an atheist for not accepting idols as gods and for teaching men."[1]

Tatishchev was misinformed about the period in which Epicurus lived,
for he was born in 342 or 341 and died in 272 or 270 B.C. Moreover,
although Epicurus was not a confirmed "atheist," he assigned a very
insignificant role to the gods in his explanation of the universe,
and, in a sense, he really educated people. These inaccuracies do not
concern us here. The fact is that Epicurus was criticized by many,
even by educated men who were more or less free from superstition
and prejudice. Most philosophical historians were quite as unjust
to him as they were toward other materialists. Tatishchev deserves
credit, therefore, for although he was not a materialist himself, he
thought it necessary to say a word in defense of Epicurus. This
praiseworthy impartiality can perhaps be explained by the fact that
he was a <u>homo</u> <u>novus</u> in questions pertaining to European education;
he had not yet learned to respect the conventional lies of the
civilized world. Our present-day opponents of materialism regard

---

[1] Tatishchev, <u>Excerpts from Historians</u>. See also his <u>Discussions</u>,
<u>op</u>. <u>cit</u>., p. 48.

such deceptions with due respect.

Interesting is the fact that, while preaching religious tolerance, Tatishchev persistently recommends to the government the adoption of stern measures against people wasting their time in useless occupations. In addition to subdividing the sciences into the two classes, "spiritual" and "natural," he also classifies them under the following five headings: 1. The necessary; 2. the useful; 3. the entertaining and the luxurious; 4. the vain and the curious; 5. the pernicious. Under pernicious sciences he lists all kinds of sorcery and magic, necromancy, astrology, horoscopy, palmistry and the like. Among the more popular kinds of magic known in Russia he lists oneirocriticism, "black magic," divination by cards, exorcism and charms. He writes as follows about those dangerous sciences: "Although these sciences are not harmful in themselves and although in the opinion of many philosophers, the death penalty for those who practice them is wrong, nevertheless such people should be subjected to physical punishment for wasting their time in useless occupations and for deceiving others."[1] This demand of physical punishment for "wasteful" spending of time reveals a worthy pupil of Peter, who insisted that even nuns, while saving their souls, should do some kind of handiwork.

---

[1] Tatishchev, Discussions, op. cit., p. 85.

Tatishchev considered epileptics to be charlatans. Popularly, individuals afflicted with epilepsy were regarded as being possessed by the devil. Tatishchev refers maliciously to Peter, who, "by means of cruel physical punishments cast out the devils in such a way that one hardly hears any longer about possessed persons, particularly in such places where there were energetic administrators

Tatishchev's Discussions gives much more than its title promises. It is almost an encyclopedia. Here is revealed this remarkable man's entire philosophy. The greater part of the Discussions deals with the seemingly simple and obvious proposition that education is necessary and useful. It would be tedious to repeat his lengthy arguments. It would not be fair, however, to blame Tatishchev for treating such a subject, since he, with the rest of the "Learned Guard," had to struggle with the stubborn conservatives, each of whom, in his particular way, clamored that the sciences were useless. In his first satire, Kantemir, too, found it necessary to condemn the enemies of the sciences.

1

Ibid. It is known that "possessed persons" continued to exist in Russia in spite of the opposition of the enlighteners ("wise heads"). Karamzin, the Russian historian, sent the following order to his overseer: "In the name of your lord notify all 'possessed persons' to quiet down and to stop their annoying practices; I order you to punish them with rods in case they do not stop, because such behavior is fraudulent and hypocritical." (P. Smirnovsky, History of Russian Literature in the 19th Century, bk. 2, St. Petersburg, 1899, p. 90.)

The old-fashioned thinkers used all possible arguments against the introduction of the sciences and even declared that education fostered disrespect for the authority of the State, as well as of the Church. For reasons quite understandable, Tatishchev analyzes this political argument very carefully. He asserts: "It is never the intelligent people who start revolts; these are always started by cunning knaves who, under cover of hypocritical piety, produce discontent and incite the mob." In support of his words he refers to the fact that Russian rebels, like Bolotnikov, Sten'ka Razin, the Strelitzes and the rabble, all belonged to the lowest classes and were entirely ignorant. Among foreign rebels we find a learned man, Cromwell. Even he had to assume "a mask of piety and simplicity" to start his revolt, but as soon as he rose to power, he destroyed the schools and threw out all the teachers and students. He thus hoped to hide his own cunning. The wise monarch seeks to have his subjects educated for the very reason that riots seldom occur in countries where the sciences flourish.[1]

During the first English Revolution the social and political demands of the non-privileged masses retained a religious character. Leaders of the 18th century enlightenment saw a danger in such an association of religion with their cause. At least this

---

[1] Tatishchev, Discussions, op. cit., pp. 65-66.

was the outlook of the French intellectuals who met at Holbach's
as the spokesmen of the revolutionary demands of the third estate.
The enlighteners naturally distrusted all political activities
carried on under the banner of the Church. This resistance to religion was aggravated in Tatishchev by his firm conviction that
every revolutionary movement is dangerous. No wonder that he
pictured Cromwell as a rascal! The "Learned Guard" was in complete
favor of absolute monarchy, and we are justified in calling Tatishchev
the chief theorist of the "Learned Guard."

When asked "What government is the best?" Tatishchev
answered "that depends on circumstances." Small nations not subject
to attack by enemies can safely adopt the democratic form of government. Great nations, however, not free from the danger of attacks
by other nations, must adopt the aristocratic form of government.
"The 'great nations' which are in constant danger of being attacked
by neighbors cannot live and prosper without an absolute monarchy."[1]

Russia owes all her successes to her dynasties. She
flourished only in times of absolute tzars. When the influence of
other princes grew, because ducal appanages became independent duke-
doms, Russia was conquered by the Tartars and the Lithuanians. Her
condition improved only under Ivan III, the "founder of the monarchy,"

---

[1]

Ibid., pp. 137-138. See also N. Popov, op. cit., pp. 116-117.

and his son and grandson. In the "Time of Troubles" (1600-1613) -
the interregnum - the boyars chose one of their own, Shuisky, as
their ruler. The law proclaimed by the boyars proved harmful.
When Shuisky was dethroned, a "government" was set up by the people.
It brought destruction and ruin to Russia, one "much worse than the
Tartar invasion." The end of this "debauchery" and the restoration
of the "old order" became possible only after "an absolute and
hereditary tzar was chosen."[1]

Feofan Prokopovich also said: "The people of Russia are
such by nature that they can be protected only by an absolute
monarchy; if any other form of government is introduced, it is impossible for them to be safe and prosperous."[2] I shall have occasion
to tell later how vigorously the "Learned Guard" rose against the
influential members of the Privy Council when they attempted to
curtail the autocratic power of Empress Anna Ivanovna. They saw
in the unlimited power of the monarch the surest guarantee of progress
and were therefore ardent advocates of the principle of absolutism.
Tatishchev is sincere when he advises his son: "Defend the honor
and power of your tzar to your last drop of blood. Never succumb
to those who praise the liberties of other states and who try to

---

[1]
 Tatishchev, Discussions, op. cit., pp. 138-139. See also N. Popov,
op. cit., p. 118.
[2]
 See his description of the "little schemes" printed in the addendum
to the Notes of Duke de Liria and Borwick, translated from the
French by D. Yezikov, St. Petersburg, 1845.

lessen the supreme power of your tzar; such an act can bring extreme misfortune to your country."[1]

Tatishchev was entirely free from "subversive tendencies" in his political activities, as well as in his social relations. He was a landlord, and he was brought up in the stern school of Peter the Great; he was severe with those of his serfs whom he found to be at fault. "Have a prison for the stubborn serfs," he wrote to his overseers. Tatishchev demanded also that his peasants do not waste their time uselessly. Since they did not work in the fields in the winter, he prescribed that they be trained as "blacksmith, wheel-maker, sheep-breeder, cooper, potter, wool-beater, feltmaker, tailor, horse-breeder, shoemaker and the like - trades of the first importance and necessity."[2] He believed that, after studying these "arts" his peasants would be able to "support themselves, particularly in the winter, without much hard work." Naturally his own interest as a landowner was not ignored by this precept. He ordered that all the peasants' children of both sexes from five to ten years must learn how to read and write. In general,

---

[1] See the _Testament_ of V. N. Tatishchev, issued under the supervision of Andrey Ostrovsky, a member of the Kazan Society of Archeology, History and Ethnography, Kazan, 1885, p. 14.

[2] See his "Brief Economic Notes relating to the Village," communicated by S. Serebryakov and printed in _Chronicles of the Imperial Society of Russian History and Antiques at Moscow_, bk. 12, Moscow, 1852.

Tatishchev favored the diffusion of knowledge among the Russian people, pointing to its importance to the state, particularly for its military needs. In such orders we see his keen foresight. Even at the present time, it would be very useful for our obscurantists to reread the pages of the Discussions relating to Tatishchev's recommendations. To be sure, he always remains a nobleman in these statements. He insists that the children of the gentry be separated from those of the commoners. It seems to him that their intermingling would be morally harmful.[1]

According to Tatishchev, one of the reasons why the Academy of Sciences founded by Peter had failed in providing proper education for the children of the nobility was the fact that they mixed freely with the children of the lower classes. Tatishchev declared that "children of noble birth will be influenced toward evil and will lose their good manners if, removed from their parents' care, they are allowed to associate with children of the common people." He also criticized the Academy because it did not "provide for such high and essential sciences as fighting with swords, horseback riding, dancing and painting." He therefore found it necessary to look for another and better school for the children

---

[1] See his Discussions, op. cit., pp. 154 and 109. In contrast, our cultured classes of the 19th century found in such communion a great deal of good (Hertzen, Boboruikin and others).

of the gentry and praised the "Cadets' Corps,"[1] founded in Anna

Ivanovna's reign.

In his Comments on the Population Census Tatishchev com-

plained that no distinction is made between the noble born and the

common people.

> Because of the absence of a law to define the rights and privi-
> leges of the higher class, every one is considered of noble
> birth. All owners of villages, clerks, sons of priests, towns-
> men and peasants having patrimonial estates, bought or acquired -
> all of them adopt some coat of arms according to their own in-
> vention and are honored because they are rich. This is a thing
> we can find nowhere else.

According to Tatishchev this tendency leads to the corrup-

tion of the people's morals. He adds:

> In view of the fact that we respect only riches and pomp, every
> one is concerned only with getting rich by whatever means possi-
> ble, and as soon as men become rich they find it easy to buy
> honors, ranks and privileges. In trying ostentatiously to gain
> an advantage over one another, they do not understand that they
> ruin not only themselves but also the State.[2]

Tatishchev says that Peter I intended to put an end to

such abuses and even decreed special privileges for the gentry as

reward for their services. After his death, however, "all was for-

gotten because of the selfishness and wickedness of those who were

entrusted with these duties."

---

[1]
Ibid., p. 112.
[2]
N. Popov, op. cit., pp. 771-772.

This was significant in several ways. In its struggle
with the boyars the gentry came out against the "right of birth."
The gentry held the opinion that the position of those serving the
government depended upon the extent of their service to the state.
Peter I encouraged this policy by forcing "birth" to the background
and making "rank" supreme. His "nestlings," of course, sympathized
with the position of the gentry. We shall observe later that such
sentiment found expression even in the belles-lettres of the time,
that is, in Kantemir's second satire. As soon as the gentry itself
entered the privileged class, it began to draw a line of demarcation
between itself and the lower classes; laws were enacted to define
the "difference" between the gentry and the commoners, Since Peter's
"nestlings" belonged to the gentry, they could not be divorced from
his inclination of their class. From this arises the duality in
conceptions so conspicuous in Tatishchev's works.

Our enlightener continued to champion the ideology of the
noble class. At the same time the theories underlying his conception
of the world - theories of Western European intellectuals - expressed
the liberal tendencies of the third estate; as such they were more
or less hostile to the "old order." The theory of "natural right"
and "natural religion" - of natural law in general - was one of
those Western ideas which Tatishchev adopted with special eagerness.
How can we explain this contradiction? We must not forget that

these theories were carried to their logical - in practice, to
their revolutionary - extremes only gradually. For this reason,
in the West, these liberal thoughts were assimilated by many
people without revolutionary inclinations whatsoever.

There were many intellectuals of this type in Germany,
but the country as a whole was less liberal than either France or
England. Pufendorf, for instance, from whom Tatishchev took so
much, was a conservative. He was a stern partisan of absolutism;
this was probably the reason why Peter the Great was pleased with
him. It is true that even the French enlighteners of the second
half of the 18th century willingly placed their trust in kings (les
princes éclairés). But Pufendorf was not only a zealous advocate
of absolutism; he was ready to compromise with some institutions,
such as slavery, which were severely criticized by the French enlighteners, and whose existence could not possibly be justified by
the law of "natural right." The basis of Pufendorf's philosophy
was: nam perpetua illa obligatio compensatur perpetua alimentorum
certitudine.

A true believer in "natural law" would reply that even
if one admitted the right of a person to give up his freedom to another for the rest of his life, one has absolutely no right to
sacrifice the freedom of his descendants. Pufendorf could not have
set forth such an argument unless he abandoned the idea of "natural
right."

There is no doubt that only such inconsistent adherents
of progressive ideas as Pufendorf were fit to be the teachers of
the ideologists among our Europeanized nobility. The consistent
ones would soon enough have found out the extent to which the socio-
political order of Russia did not conform to "natural law," originated in the West in the course of the struggle against the "old
order."

In France the movement for emancipation of the third
estate was incomparably stronger than in Germany. As a result the
French educators were considerably bolder and more consistent than
their German colleagues. Russian educators followed either the
former or the latter, according to their attitude toward "actual
conditions in Russia," as the phrase ran in the 19th century. They
leaned upon the Germans when they accepted reality, and as soon as
they rebelled against it, they gravitated towards the French. The
apparent exceptions to this rule serve only to strengthen it (the
history of Voltaire's influence upon the more or less educated
Russians proves it). Some individuals (Radishchev, Byelinsky)
showed leanings toward the French in those periods of their lives
when they held radical views, and to the Germans when they com-
promised with "reality" (Byelinsky) or, at least, when they were
beginning to become tired of struggling for their ideals (Radishchev).

Let us see how Tatishchev treats the doctrine of "natural
law." He reasons thus: "Liberty, given to us by nature, is so useful and necessary that no other happiness may be compared to it."

This almost sounds like a revolutionary call. But this almost revolutionary statement is accompanied by important reservations.
Liberty brings benefit to people only when they employ it wisely.
Not all people are capable of doing so. For his own benefit a
child must be kept under the care of his parents. From this concept of parental tutelage follows the power of the monarch, whom
his subjects must obey. A servant also obeys his master. Although the power of the father and the power of the monarch are
given by nature itself, the authority of the master over his servant
rests upon a contract:

> For instance, a person unable to provide himself with a dwell-
> ing, food, clothes or protection against his enemies makes an
> agreement with another person who has more than he can use
> of these necessities. The servant promises to give his services
> and his freedom in exchange for food, clothing, shelter and
> protection against violence. Thus, by giving up his freedom,
> the servant has no personal liberty left.[1]

In statements of this kind, Tatischev frequently comes
very close to Pufendorf, but he disagrees with him in regard to
the origin of the monarch's power. The German writer traces its
origin to a contract, while the Russian explains it as a result of
natural law, as in the case of parental tutelage. Whence comes this
difference? As can be seen, Tatishchev found that the contract
theory cannot serve as a sound theoretical foundation for the power
of the Russian tzar. We cannot but agree that the contract theory

---

[1]
 Tatishchev, _Discussions_, op. cit., pp. 139-141.

did not prove reliable in this case. It carried in itself the most
radical deductions made later by French revolutionaries, but from
the standpoint of "natural law" this theory was no more suitable
to justify the power of the Russian tzar than the servant's dependence upon his master. Nevertheless, Tatishchev utilized the
contract theory exactly for that purpose. Sketching the form of
the agreement whereby one party promises to serve and the other to
provide food, clothing, shelter and protection, Tatishchev adds:
"In this agreement we find the origin of the servant's or serf's
dependence." Historically he is right. Servitude is based upon
such a "contract." The fact is that in their efforts to be logically consistent, the "enlighteners" were not satisfied with mere
historical explanations of such dependence; they had either to condemn it or to find an adequate justification, satisfactory to reason
and logic.

It is quite remarkable that while propounding the necessity
of "the curtailment of slavery" in his Discussions, Tatishchev
did not mention a word about the legal provisions sanctioning serfdom. He was seemingly cognizant of the fact that even the historical
origin of slavery could not be satisfactorily explained by the contract theory. This was not all. He generally denied - I repeat,
in the Discussions - the justice of "slavery or serfdom," although
he did call the children of serfs the "children of slaves." Slavery

is a product of violence, and violence does not beget righteousness. "So long as man has by nature the freedom to protect and defend himself," Tatishchev reasoned, "he must cease to tolerate being denied his personal freedom as soon as the opportunity to be freed arises."[1] From this it follows logically that if the lower class is forced to slavery by the upper class, the former has the natural right to rise against its enslavers. It is true that here, too, Tatishchev makes reservations: "Even this must be done with caution, for if I, a captive of the enemy or a band of brigands, dared to exact revenge and liberate myself by employing my limited strength, I would be the cause of my own undoing." This, of course, is correct. What interests me is not a discussion of the conditions favorable to the uprising of the enslaved against their enslavers, but the question of whether we must recognize such liberation as justifiable. The question was answered affirmatively by Tatishchev in the most emphatic manner.

One should not think that Tatishchev was, even in theory, against serfdom as proclaimed by the laws. In another passage he expressly favors it. Not being able to justify it on the ground of "natural law," he transferred the matter to another field. He appealed to politics. "The liberty of peasants and serfs is useful in other countries," he says. "Such liberty might have brought

---

[1] *Ibid.*, p. 141.

benefit to our country also at the time of Ivan the Terrible,
particularly in those instances in which the 'dissolute landlords'
oppressed their men. That liberty does not conform to our absolu-
tistic form of government, and the abolition of the deep-rooted
custom of serfdom is unsafe."

The example of Tatishchev shows us that the educated
noblemen of Great Russia, products of Peter's reforms, were well
acquainted with the socio-political situation of Western Europe;
they knew how to combine, in their theories, their interests as
landlords with the interests of an absolute monarchy. Although
their reference to the safety of the state appeared for a long time
to be convincing both to themselves and to the representatives of
the government, it did not furnish any logical justification of
legal serfdom from the viewpoint of "natural law." The obstacle
upon which Tatishchev stumbled remained unmoved. And this was not
the only one.

The Europeanized ideologists of the Russian nobility had
to explain and defend the privileged status of their class with
the help of theories not very appropriate for this purpose because
of their radical nature. It is possible to say, of course, that
in the West there were theories more conservative than, for instance,
the theory of "natural law." In the first place, however, the conservative theories of the West were too mild compared to those developed during the emancipation movement. Secondly, and this is

the crux of the matter, one very important socio-political factor prevented "Peter's nestlings" from assimilating the teachings of the Western European conservatives. The latter's teachings defended the political demands of the upper classes, demands which Russia's central government did not even want to hear, particularly during the time of Ivan IV and Peter I. The Western European bourgeoisiq while fighting the secular and clerical aristocracies, supported absolutism; the theories propounded by these ideologists seemed to be better adapted to the political order of Russia. It remained for the French Revolution to disclose the consequences inherent in these theories.

Even if for the time being these theories seemed more suitable to Russian political conditions, nevertheless, no serious logical argument could be deduced from them in defense of our "original" institutions such as "legal serfdom." Consequently, the position of the enlightened ideologists of the Russian nobility was in the end shaken. That is why later they struggled so unsuccessfully against those Russians who appeared - although frequently only in their youth - as advocates of the revolutionary teachings of the West.

Let us return to Tatishchev. The characterization of Tatishchev as the ideologist of the Russian nobility would not be complete without pointing out his solicitude for the peasants. This concern is expressed on almost every page of his Economic Notes.

He introduced for his serfs not only jails, but also schools and
bathhouses.[1] His foreman and bailiff had to take good care that
"every married peasant had two draught horses, two oxen, fifteen
sheep (ten ewes and five rams), ten pigs, two pairs of geese, ten
hens. Those who wanted to have more, should be permitted to do so;
but in no case should they be allowed to have less." For the old
and sick peasants he established an asylum in which they were "on
the board of their master." The solicitous attention of the landlord was turned even to the household utensils of his peasants.
Every one of them was obliged to have "dishes, plates, knives,
forks, tin spoons, saltcellars, glasses, table covers, towels,
shelves or cupboards, tin buckets and dippers." Peasants who, because of their carelessness, failed to possess all these things
were severely punished by being assigned as laborers without pay
to the households of deserving peasants, who made use of the land
and labor of these inefficient men and also paid their taxes.
"Idlers" remained under such tutelage until they were given a "good
recommendation."

It goes without saying that Tatishchev's solicitude for
his peasants' welfare was that of a noble slave-owner who knows
the value of a "living" piece of property and also how to exploit

---

[1]
"Two large bathhouses (one for men and one for women) to be
operated on alternate Saturday afternoons." Sovremennik (Contemporary), p. 20.

its labor. He strictly orders his bailiff to watch "that no loaf-
ing be permitted during the busy summer months and that no leave
of absence be granted to any one without special justification."[1]
Tatishchev, at least, secured for his peasants their material well-
being, and this few other serf-owners did.

The most notable thing about Tatishchev is his opinion
of women. The singularity of his attitude is revealed partly by
his concern about the literacy of both sexes among his peasants.
It is shown still more in Tatishchev's advice to his son: "Keep
in mind particularly that your wife is not your slave. She should
be a true friend and veritable helpmate, and you must be the same
to her."[2]

Although he attended to his duties carefully, Tatishchev
did not want to be obsequious; he looked upon courtiers with distrust. He does not recommend to his son to seek "service at the
court," for "there jealousy, flattery, artfulness, hatred and deceit
obscure all virtues. Many seek to obtain their advancement by in-
trigue, without considering that if they destroy the innocent, they
themselves will perish at the hand of God."[3]

1
Ibid., p. 20.
2
Tatishchev, Testament, p. 13.
3
Ibid., p. 20.

Bersen Beklemishev, the boyar, once said to Maxim Griech:
"The land that changes its customs cannot exist for very long."
This was the attitude of Muscovite Russia. "Peter's nestlings" had
a different view. While remaining conservative in whatever concerned the foundations of socio-political life, they nevertheless
approved changes in established customs. Tatishchev even evolved
a complete theory of progress. Although he did not expect to attain
the "golden age" in the immediate future, he would probably have
agreed with Saint-Simon's statement that there is no reason why
the golden age cannot be achieved. "When we study the knowledge
and the mentality of ancient nations," he says, "we can conclude
that those peoples, just as any human individual, attained nothing
in their infancy, very little in their youth, and only a few useful
accomplishments in their maturity."[1]

The French intellectuals of the 18th century frequently
judged the progress of society by comparing it with the development
of the individual. The socialistic Utopians of the first half of
the 19th century adopted this analogy. Saint-Simon employed this
method when he attempted to formulate a law concerning the three
stages in the mental development of humanity.[2]

---

[1]
Tatishchev, _Discussions_, op. cit., p. 38.
[2]
More details about this may be found in the third chapter of
Plekhanov's _The Development of Monism in History_. (_Works_, vol. 7.)

In his way of thinking and of reasoning about the "natural law," Tatishchev reveals himself as a true enlightener.[1] Finally, Tatishchev appears as an enlightener in his general views upon the fundamental causes of the evolution of history. He explains this movement in terms of "mental development." What is mental development? It is the gathering and dissemination of knowledge. What is knowledge? This question was answered by our Russian enlightener during the first half of the 18th century, but not in the same way as the French enlighteners answered it fifty years later.

The French enlighteners viewed religion negatively. Hence in their eyes religious conceptions had nothing in common with scientific ideas. Progress in education, according to them, must inevitably undermine religious belief and diminish its influence. Tatishchev did not view religion in the same light; as we have already seen, he respected it. In his philosophy of history much credit is given to the development of religious conceptions as a means of enlightenment. "The first factor in the development of the mind," he says, "is the invention of the art of writing; the second, Christ's advent and teachings; the third, the invention

---

[1] Chronologically he was the first Russian enlightener.

of the printing press."[1]

After writing these lines, Tatishchev, as though recall-
ing the teachings of the Church in respect to the relationship of
the New Testament to the Old, hastened to add: "It appears that
the period before the invention of writing and the Ten Commandments
may be compared to the childhood of man."[2]

According to Dr. Lerch, Tatishchev had his own views on
religion. This caused many to think that he was unorthodox.[3] In
his Testament our author emphatically denies that he is an atheist
and a heretic. I have remarked above that the secular element in
his writings differentiates him from the learned men before Peter I;
yet he did not sever all ties with religion. He was inclined to
compromise with it even in his philosophy of history. In this

---

1

Compare with his "Introduction" to Russian History, bk. 1, pt. 1,
Moscow, 1768, p. XXVII: "The greatest factors in the development
of the mind I consider to be the alphabet, Christ's teachings and
the printing of books. Writing made it possible to preserve in
memory for all time that which had been talked about and to transfer
our thoughts to men who are far away from us. The Saviour's advent brought to men the recognition of the Creator and the true
obligation of man to God, to himself and to his fellow men. The
printing of books and everyone's freedom to use them gave to the
world the greatest instrument for the dissemination of knowledge.
Through printing, our knowledge and also the number of useful books
increased."

2

Tatishchev, Discussions, op. cit., p. 38. See the article of
Bestuzhev-Ryumin, (p. 27), "Vasily Nikitich Tatishchev," The Old
and the New Russia, 1875, chapter 2, p. 261. According to Tatishchev
there are four stages in the development of the human race: the
fourth extends from the invention of printing to the present time.

3

Ibid., p. 261.

matter, our educated ideologist of the nobility followed the moderate German enlighteners, who saw in religion a divine means of "educating mankind," rather than the extreme radical French enlighteners, who regarded religion as a serious obstacle to the development of the human mind.

The difference between the radical and the moderate enlighteners may be observed only where nonheathen religions are concerned. In regard to heathen religions the moderate thinkers of the 18th century shared the opinion of the radicals. Tatishchev wrote, for instance, that "in order to induce people, through fear, to lead pious and honest lives, Pythagoras developed the theory of the transmigration of the soul according to each creature's behavior."[1] Diderot himself would have agreed with this interpretation of Tatishchev's. Religious dogmas are usually enunciated by crafty men with a view to exploiting their fellow men, but sometimes for the purpose of "restraining" them from doing evil. This theory of the 18th century enlighteners was adopted even by some of the prominent socialistic Utopians of the 19th century; from this conception sprang the "New Christianity" of Saint-Simon and the "True Christianity" of Cabet.

In the normal development of the historical process, however, the accumulation and dissemination of knowledge play the leading role. This process of dissemination depends to a large extent

---

[1] The History of Russia, bk. 2, p. 383. While discussing this subject, the author employs the vocabulary of Valkh.

upon the "assiduity" of the people and upon the "benevolence of the government." Of course, the words "benevolence of the government" had to be added by Tatishchev, a true 18th century enlightener.

A man may lack knowledge because of his own laziness and unwillingness, and also because of neglect by his parents. On the other hand, by diligence and application, some can gain much more than others. As it is with individuals, so is it with countries: because of their efficient schools and the adequate protection provided by their rulers some are more advanced than others.

For instance, great progress was made by the sciences as a result of the efforts of Henry VIII and Queen Elizabeth in England, and of Henry IV and Louis XIV in France.[1]

It is Tatishchev's method of reasoning - I ask the reader to notice this fact particularly - rather than his individual conceptions that makes him the leader of our numerous enlighteners, occupying, as he did for a long time, a predominant place in our literature. If he was the first important representative of that type of enlightener, Chernyshevsky and Dobrolyubov were its most prominent, most brilliant and most influential figures.

As is known, Tatishchev's works have been reviewed and properly evaluated by a competent specialist, S. M. Soloviev. The latter wrote about Tatishchev's historical works as follows:

---

[1] Tatishchev, Discussions, op. cit., p. 121. Elsewhere Tatischev states categorically that "all acts are affected by reason or lack of reason."

"Tatishchev's merit consists mostly in the fact that he
was the first to use the scientific approach: he collected material,
reviewed it, compared it with old archives and added to it geographical, ethnological and chronological notes. He pointed out
many important questions that served as topics for subsequent scholars
and collected various works of old and modern writers concerning
the early condition of the country known later as Russia. In a
word, he was a pioneer and furnished the material to his fellow
countrymen for the study of Russia's history... Last but not least,
Tatishchev deserves credit for preserving much information taken
from the archives which would perhaps have been lost to us forever;
the importance of these data is increasing from day to day."[1]

Tatishchev also contributed a great deal to the history
of Russian jurisprudence. According to Soloviev, Tatishchev appears
to be a pioneer in this field too, as the first editor and commen-
tator of codes. He compiled the Russian laws and the Code of
Tzar Ivan, with annotations. In the notes to the Code, Soloviev
saw the first attempt to explain our ancient legal terms.

And, as if this were not enough, this remarkable man
wrote also the first books on Russian geography.[2]

---

[1] "The Writers of Russian History of the 18th Century," in the
Collected Works of S. M. Soloviev, pp. 1346-1347. Compare The Main
Currents of Russian Historical Thought, P. N. Milyukov, Moscow,
1897, pp. 15-23.

[2] According to the comment of A. N. Pipin, Tatishchev first found it
necessary (for historiographical purposes) to study "the life of
the people with their peculiarities, customs and traditions."
(The History of Russian Literature, vol. 3, p. 336.)

Because of these achievements, Soloviev justly
allotted to Tatishchev a place on a level with Michael Lomonosov,
"the most honorable place in the history of early Russian science."[1]

Like all "Peter's nestlings," Tatishchev was active in
various practical pursuits: he was a mining engineer, an artillery
officer and an administrator. He served intelligently and diligently, but as mentioned before, he was never servile. During the
rule of Anna, Tatischev was prosecuted and suffered bureaucratic vexations almost until
his death because he was disliked by Biron. It is not our task to
find out whether or not he was as blameless as he thought himself
to be. At that time, outstanding persons looked differently on
practical activity than do our leaders today.

3. ANTIOCH DIMITRY KANTEMIR[2]

The problem of the purity of the Russian language did not
escape Tatishchev's attention. Of course, he understood clearly
that it was impossible to dispense with the philological influence
of foreign languages. He warned, however, that "among foreign loan
words there are many whose equivalent we have in our own language;

[1] Soloviev, op. cit., p. 1350.

[2] 1709-1744. His father was a Moldavian prince, who, in 1711 became a subject of Peter the Great. The elder Prince Kantemir was
a distinguished scholar; he wrote several books on Moldavia and
Turkey in Greek and Rumanian. His mother was a well-educated Greek.
Young Kantemir was a "man of service." From 1731 until 1738 he
served as minister resident in London. In 1738 he was named ambassador to Paris where he remained until his death. - Translator's
Note.

120

these are more understandable to our people. It would be unwise,
therefore, to replace these by unnecessary foreign expressions."[1]
Unfortunately, this great truth is often ignored by Russian writers,
including many of the present era. The followers of the democratic
camp must remember that the working masses do not learn foreign
languages, either in Russia or elsewhere in the world.

Literature as such did not particularly attract Tatishchev. It was another member of the "Learned Guard," Prince Antioch
Dimitry Kantemir, who became a connoisseur in this field.

His satires may be called classical in the sense that we
became acquainted with them while still at school. In addition to
his satires, Kantemir wrote "songs," "letters," various short verses
and sometimes such works as the above-mentioned Petrida, as well as
A Speech in Honor of Her Majesty Anna Ivanova.[2] Besides, he made
translations in verse (Anacreon, Horace) and in prose (Fontenelle,
Montesquieu). Finally, we must mention his eleven philosophical
Letters on Nature and Man, preserved in a very poor edition. In
all of these works of Kantemir's, there is very interesting material
relating to the history of Russian social thought.

---

[1]
Tatishchev, Discussions, op. cit., p. 95-96.
[2]
Alas! also written in poetical form!

To begin with, Kantemir, like Tatishchev, not only wrote many works but also served in the government of his country. Almost all the Russian writers of that time did the same thing; they were servants of the tzar. As a man interested in literature, Kantemir was more enthusiastic about composing his heavy verses or translating foreign authors than about preparing his official reports. He himself must have been aware of his shortcomings in this respect, since most of those service men considered service to the state more important than literature.

Kantemir frankly expressed the same opinion in his "Letter" headed "To My Verses," written in 1743, when he was preparing his poetical attempts for printing. Our distinguished satirist anticipated criticism of his waste of time on work suited neither to his rank nor his age, by addressing his verses as follows: "...You will try to convince the people that you did not harm my youth or interfere with my most important responsibilities, and that duty has always found me ready to serve my country...."

Kantemir tried in vain to argue with those who had very little use for literature. All Russian writers who served the state found themselves in an awkward position: charged with a serious task, they neglected it from time to time for more pleasant distractions. Their superiors did not fail to impress on them the necessity of choosing between service to the state and writing.

Fortunately for Russian letters and for Russia's social development, devotion to literature, among the more brilliant and gifted, was much stronger than their interest in official routine work.

It is known that Kantemir's parents were not of Russian origin and that Kantemir left Russia while still a young man, at the age of twenty-two, and died abroad in a social milieu very unlike the Russia of those days. Still he adopted and retained the conceptions of the Russian nobility, the most educated group in the Russia of this period. Such is the power of early impressions. For instance, Western civilization, which was so dear to Kantemir, did not make him question the legality of serfdom. He described this bondage as something quite natural. Sometimes he even pictured it as being to the best advantage of the peasants themselves.

In answer to Prokopovich's verse, "The Little Shepherd Cries during the Many Rainy Days," he describes his own losses in this way:

> Goats I had - a few;
> It is well known:
> From them my modest fortune grew.
> But they are gone!
> George and his friends took them way from me.[1]

"George" was the Bishop George Dashkov of Rostov, belonging to the group hostile to Prokopovich and Kantemir; by "goats" Kantemir meant serfs. These were taken away from our poet not by

---

[1] "Epodos consolatoria."

Bishop Dashkov but by the Supreme Privy Council, which decided that
the estates left by the elder Prince Dimitry Kantemir belonged to
our poet's younger brother, Constantine.[1]

Of course, the bondage of the serfs ("goats") was legally
recognized. On the other hand, young Kantemir had a very clear
conception of "natural law." In a note to his first satire he says:
"Natural law is a rule prescribed for us by nature itself; this law
is binding, and no society can live without it." Manifestly, the
question of the serfs' bondage should be considered in terms of
this rule, "which is binding and prescribed for us by nature itself." In Kantemir's works, however, we do not notice any deep
signs of such a conviction. In this respect his philosophy remained
almost untouched by criticism. In his second satire (On Envy and
Pride in Ill-natured Noblemen) he rises against the cruel treatment
of servants and even says: "The flesh of your servant is the same
as yours." This acknowledgment of the equality of the flesh of the
nobleman and the serf does not, however, arouse Kantemir's doubt as
to the moral correctness of serfdom. He even approves corporeal
punishment for servants by their masters, demanding only that it be
deserved and just. "Even the guilty should be treated with leniency,"
he says in the footnote to the 290th verse of the satire under dis-

---

[1]
At that time, the so-called rule of primogeniture, a misnomer with
regard to the Russian law of inheritance, was in force. Prince
Dimitry Kantemir left it to the government to decide which of his
sons was to inherit his estates.

cussion, "and if punishment is necessary, it should be administered with but one purpose: to mend the ways of the guilty and to prevent others from committing crime, and not to satisfy one's anger toward a defenseless man."

Of course, the writer who gave this advice for punishing serfs was far more human than most of the other masters. Yet even he accepted the ownership of human chattels and did not protest against the inhumane foundation of the institution of slavery; he wanted only to introduce an element of humanity into the system.

To conclude my remarks about Kantemir's attitude toward the serfs, I shall say that in all his pastorals he always pictured the serfs as crude and stupid. In one of his Letters on Nature and Man - a discourse on the power of the mind over the body - he states, among other things, that this power belongs not only to the privileged but also to the "simple and unimportant peasant, because he can move his body as well as a scientist skilled in anatomy."[1] On the other hand, he says that "our village games are as crude and hideous as the early Latin comedies of the common people."[2] He gives an explanation of this crudity: it is not difficult to visualize the primitive existence described in these Latin folksongs;

---

[1]
  Prince A. D. Kantemir's Works, Letters and Selected Translations, edited and published by P. A. Efremov, St. Petersburg, 1869, vol. 2, p. 61.
[2]
  Ibid., vol. 1, p. 529, footnote.

they picture the life of the peasants, deprived, as they were, of all beauty and joy."[1]

The late V. Stoyunin refused to recognize Kantemir as a partisan of any political faction. "We may call him a devotee of science," he wrote: "this, is what identifies Kantemir with the epoch of Peter the Great...."[2] This opinion of Stoyunin's is not correct. In consonance with his social outlook, Kantemir, together with other members of the "Learned Guard," took a definite political stand, and it was because of this that he was identified with the epoch of Peter the Great. Aside from his political views, too, we must keep in mind that the writer's philosophy always bore the stamp of the social relations of his time, no matter how much he valued the sciences. In fact, Kantemir held the cause of enlightenment in great esteem.

---

[1] _Ibid._, p. 528. Here he adds that "we, too, have many such folksongs created by the common people." He quotes the beginning of one of the many popular songs about Tzar Ivan IV:

It happened in the past, and in the good old days, in the reign of the famous Tzar, Ivan Vasilyevich. The Sovereign Tzar decided to get married...

The reader probably agrees that Kantemir's "songs" would sound much better and be much more readable if they resembled such "creations of our common people."

[2] See Stoyunin's introductory article to the _Works of Kantemir_, vol. 1, p. XLV.

This distinguished diplomat,[1] who wrote that serious men should engage in literature only during their spare time, did not lose interest in books until a few days before his death; this interest lost, he decided that the time had come to die. Like Tatishchev, he remained, to his last days, the ideologist of the Europeanized Russian nobility. It is for this reason that his world outlook becomes of interest to the historian of Russian social thought. Kantemir's example shows, perhaps even more clearly than Tatishchev's, how the educated representatives of the Russian privileged class adapted to their own use the very ideas which were worked out by the underprivileged classes of the West in their struggle against the clergy and nobility.

The reader's attention has already been drawn to the fact that in Tatishchev, that remarkable exponent of the post-reform period, the secular element predominated over the theological one. The same should also be said of Kantemir. He wrote with intense interest on morality, but he never invoked the lives of the saints, as was customary with the Russian moralists of the Moscow period, but turned rather to lay authors, even to such pagan writers as Horace. But those of his contemporaries who, seeing in his views the predominance of the lay element over the theological, considered

---

[1] He died while a member of the Supreme Privy Council, on March 31, 1744, at the age of thirty-five.

him an atheist, were in error. He was even less of an atheist
than Tatishchev. That Kantemir had been under the influence of
religion since his early years can be seen from his first work,
The Symphony of the Psalm Book, published in 1727. The basic
problems of religion continued to interest him to his last days.
His letters[1] dealing with nature and man attempt to defend the religious creeds which had already begun to weaken in the West under
the influence of the philosophy of enlightenment. It is true, however, that here, as well as in the field of morality, he appealed
to lay authors. In his persistent defense of his religious creed,
he looked neither to theology nor to the Holy Scriptures, but to
philosophy.

Kantemir's introduction and footnotes to Fontenelle's
book clearly show how difficult it was to write on philosophical
questions in the Russia of that time. "We have not the necessary
books on philosophy," he said; "therefore, we are short of the explanations needed for the understanding of the philosophical sciences."
He would have been justified if he had said: "We have not even worked
out a clear, intelligible philosophical terminology." Kantemir had
to begin with the explanation of what is called philosophy. He fulfilled his duty as enlightener patiently and scrupulously, forced,

---

[1] These letters were written by Kantemir to a Russian lady during
his seclusion, while he was taking treatments in a health resort.
In unfolding their philosophical views, Russian writers liked to
appeal to women.

as he was, to begin literally with the ABC's.

"Philosophy," he explained, "is a Greek word.   In Russian
it means 'fondness for wisdom.' This general term refers to the
thorough and clear knowledge of natural and spiritual matters,
achieved by means of diligent reasoning and investigation." Then
he states that philosophy is divided into "logic, ethics, physics
(sic!) and metaphysics." This exposition is followed, of course,
by a number of new explanations:

> Logic teaches us how to argue about things and how to demon-
> strate to others known truths.

> Ethics teaches us good behavior, that is, it helps us to dis-
> tinguish between good and evil. It also formulates rules on
> how to avoid ill temper and on how to become virtuous.

> Physics or natural philosophy teaches us the causes and circum-
> stances of all phenomena in nature.

> Metaphysics or supernatural philosophy give us knowledge of
> the foundations of society, and of abstract entities such as
> soul, spirit and God.[1]

Stoyunin observed that Kantemir's translation of Fontenelle
may be considered the first step in the development of a Russian
philosophical terminology. This is true. Kantemir, as shown by
this scholar, had mastered well the difficulties of philosophical
language. He introduced such expressions as "element" and "media,"
and translated into Russian the Greek word "idea" to mean "conception."
Poor Kantemir! He had to explain to his readers not only the mean-

---

[1]
Kantemir, op. cit., vol. 2, pp. 392-393. In general, Kantemir's
style is much better in his prose than in his verses.

ings of such words as "system," "substance," but also that "Paris
is the capital of France," and that the word "theatre" is of Greek
origin and that it means "the place where comedians do their acting."
The readers who needed such explanations were, of course, also in
need of footnotes from which they could learn, for instance, that
Pythagoras, "the head of the Italian School, was a Greek philosopher
during the reign of Tarquin, the last king of Rome, 586 B.C.," and
that Aristotle was "the head of the Peripatetic School and was born
in 384 B.C. at Stagira, a Macedonian city." Some of these footnotes
are valuable to us now, as they give an insight into Kantemir's own
philosophical ideas. It will be of interest to a reader of our time
to know what Kantemir thought of the philosophy of Pythagoras:

> It was incomprehensible, because Pythagoras believed in the
> supernatural, attached mystical significance to numbers and
> explained some natural phenomena by the strange influence of
> mythical beings.

Evidently our author preferred Aristotle to all other
Greek philosophers. According to Kantemir, Aristotle was "the first
to put order into philosophy and to lay the foundation for this
science." Following Fontenelle, Kantemir pointed out the weak side
of Aristotle's method in these words: "Since it is impossible for
any one human being to know all natural phenomena, Aristotle ascribed
to those he did not comprehend the influence of secret forces."

In discussing modern thinkers, Kantemir speaks admiringly
of the works of Descartes, whom he believes to have supplemented the
philosophy of Aristotle: "Thanks to the contributions of Descartes

and those who followed him we are able to understand more clearly
all existing things." According to Kantemir, Descartes' greatest
service consists in "that he uses mathematical, that is, incontrovertible arguments in his philosophy and that he explains all
phenomena clearly or admits that he does not understand them."[1] He
says this in a footnote, but in a letter to Baron Korf, the head
of the Academy of Sciences, Kantemir requests that the error that
crept into the footnote be corrected: "L'article 'Descartes', il
faut ôter la description de sa philosophie, car elle convient plus
a M. Newton." Apparently, Baron Korf did not carry out Kantemir's
request because the article on Descartes is printed without any
notations, at least in Efremov's edition.

What Kantemir wrote on Descartes' philosophy was, according to his own words, more applicable to the ideas of Newton. This
is due to the fact that his ideas of the history and methods of
philosophic thought were not clearly worked out at the time he anno-
tated his translation of Fontenelle. We must not be surprised at
this, for his knowledge of philosophy was less extensive than his
knowledge of literature. Apparently he became acquainted with
philosophy not through the originals but through second-hand sources.
Indeed, Kantemir did not boast of being a specialist in the field.
Although the article on Descartes is "more applicable to Newton

[1]
Ibid., p. 405.

than to Descartes," nevertheless it is very interesting. His request addressed to the philosophers "to explain clearly the actions of all things or to acknowledge openly that the cause is unknown" is very characteristic of such an enlightener as Kantemir.

It is most remarkable that Kantemir himself forgot this criterion when it came to the theories which he adduced in defense of his religious beliefs. He resorted continually to that method which, according to his own words, constituted the weak side of Aristotle's. In the main, his Letters on Nature and Man contained little more than references to some kind of "mysterious force." This is easy to understand. Even among the progressive French enlighteners of the second half of the 18th century and even among the promoters of the great French Revolution, only a few undaunted thinkers shut out "mysterious force" from their conceptions of the universe. It would not be just to demand such boldness from the Russian intellectuals of the first half of the 18th century.

It is well known that Newton, the mathematician, peremptorily refused to apply hypothetical methods to his scientific inquiries. Nevertheless he remained to his last days a religious man; in his contemplation of the world he could not do without the "hypothesis of God's existence." Kantemir was not inclined to blame the famous English naturalist for this inconsistency. On the contrary, Kantemir believed in God, and, seeing a weakening of faith in God among the most progressive countries of Europe, he

turned to those philosophical arguments which defended the existence
of God. The weakest of them, namely, the so-called physico-theological proof, seemed to him to be the most convincing. Kantemir
does not hesitate to expound and repeat this, in more ways than one,
in his philosophical letters.[1]

As an example of his thinking, I shall quote at length from
his eighth letter. He summarizes all his previous reasonings as
follows: "We saw divine signs of the living God in everything
that is called the creation of nature. When we put aside all superfluous and needless things, we see, first of all, the hand which
holds together all parts of the world, heaven and earth, stars,

---

[1]
Besides, in speaking of the physico-theological proof of the existence of God, one must remember that this was generally the
fashion in the 18th century, and there was a special reason for
it. "It seems to have reconciled the strictest demands of science
relating to nature with the needs of religious sentiment." (Wilhelm
Windelband, Die Geschichte der neueren Philosophie, Leipzig, 1911,
p. 309.) Windelband adds correctly: "This view was, more than
any other, adapted to replacing historical revelation by natural
revelation, thus forcing confessional denominations to give way
to a conviction of scientific reason." Even this moderated opinion
must have appeared monstrous from the point of view of traditional
conceptions. We know that Kantemir was suspected of being a non-
believer. A Report on Books Written against Our Faith and Morality,
was presented by the Russian Synod to the Empress Elizabeth in
1757. The Synod asked for an edict forbidding, under penalty of
severe punishment, any one from writing or printing anything
contrary to the Holy Faith and in conflict with accepted beliefs.
The Synod also asked that Prince Kantemir's translation of
Fontenelle be confiscated and turned over to the Synod. (A. Kantemir,
Works, vol. 2, p. 446.)

A partisan of Peter the Great and his reforms, M. P. Avramov,
criticized Kantemir severely for his recognition of the Copernican
system. (Chistovich, op. cit., p. 692.)

living and growing beings and our bodies and minds. Everything
shows order, exact measure, great wisdom, ingenuity, the omnipotent superior spirit (Supreme Being) ruling us. This spirit,
like   the   soul   of the whole world, leads everything
quietly and imperceptibly from the beginning to the end."[1]

Kantemir further declares that the wisdom in every living
thing is manifest even to "an unintelligent person"; if only we
could penetrate the secrets of all creation and understand how the
laws of physics work, we could behold the most precious parts of
every living thing and realize finally the perfect operation of
the art of mechanics. We need not do this since it is clear to us
that "God is the One, the Omnipotent who exercises His power over
us; human happiness depends on Him only, and for this reason I must
obey His will and worship His divine determination of my life."[2]

Our author, it should be noted, realizes full well that
such "arguments" as these may be criticized. He says in the next
letter:

> There were philosophers in the past and they may have modern
> followers who will tell me that my arguments about an in-
> telligent order and the wisdom of nature are mere sophisms.
> They will say that all nature serves the wants of men and
> that I have concluded incorrectly that nature is purposely
> designed for man, and also that I deceive myself in reason-
> ing as I do because I look for, and therefore find, things

1
 Kantemir, op. cit., vol. 1, p. 81.
2
 Ibid., vol. 2, pp. 81-82.

which do not exist.[1]

Kantemir does not go deeply into this objection. He only defends himself by repeating the same physico-theological argument. He asks: "What is to be said of a man who, eager to understand the most subtle philosophy and to be known as a philosopher, argues and insists that his existence is but an accident, and that the peace of mankind has been in no way improved by intelligence and close application?...."[2]

Here it would not be difficult to accuse him of "sophism."[3] Indeed, in trying to prove the accuracy of the physico-theological argument, Kantemir presupposes that it is sound. My problem is not to quarrel with Kantemir, who, at any rate, has the merit of being one of the first Russian writers treating purely philosophical questions. It is rather to help the reader to get a correct picture of his philosophic outlook. Therefore, I shall not criticize these views but merely record them.

---

[1] Ibid., vol. 2, p. 82.

[2] Ibid., vol. 2, p. 83.

[3] Spinoza had uncovered the weakness of the physico-theological argument. People find in nature many things that help to answer their purposes. Therefore they look at nature from the point of view of their own interest. Spinoza says: "Now having considered things as means, they cannot believe them to be self-created; but they must conclude from the means which they are wont to prepare for themselves, that there is some governor or governors, endowed with human freedom, who take care of all things for them and make all things for their use." (Spinoza, Ethics, London and Toronto, 1934, p. 31.) It is not known whether Kantemir was acquainted with these thoughts of Spinoza's. Besides, if he did know them, he had to discard them, because they did not fit into his philosophical system.

Of course, our author considered the idea of God to be
innate in man. He wrote: "This idea is always with me, and in
reality it was born with me."[1] It is clear also that he recognized
the effectiveness of two substances in man, and that this effectiveness served him as a new testimony of God's existence. He says:
"The nature of my soul is different from that of my body. Who has
united these different substances and continues to correlate all
their actions? That could be accomplished only by a Superior Being
who unified these different entities into their highest perfection."[2]
This is not stated well,[3] but the reasoning is carried out in the
spirit of Descartes, whose philosophy left a deep impression on
Kantemir's mind.

Kantemir also borrowed from Descartes his doctrine of
free will:

> My will depends on me and no one else, and I am responsible
> for not wanting what another may want. If I want something I
> am free also not to want it, and if I do not want something,
> I am free to want it. My will is free...I feel that my
> rational will acts in case of things causing pleasure or pain;[4]
> I do not know any other cause of volition but the will itself.

---

[1] Kantemir, op. cit., vol. 2, p. 76.

[2] Ibid., vol. 2, p. 79.

[3] We must not forget that the copies of Kantemir's philosophical
letters which have come down to us are in a very bad condition.

[4] Ibid. Spinoza said: "Men think themselves free inasmuch as they
are conscious of their volitions and desires, and as they are
ignorant of the causes by which they are led to wish and desire,
they do not even dream of their existence." (Spinoza, op. cit.,
p. 30.) As we see, Kantemir did not "dream" of these causes
either.

Tho question of tho responsibility of people for their acts is solved very easily with the help of such an interpretation of free will. Kantemir argues:

> This will in my behavior makes me responsible for all my acts; I can havo no excuso for wishing anything bad, and, on tho other hand, I deserve ovory praise for having good intentions. This is the very foundation of human dignity or of human shame. It justifies either punishment or reward; from this come inspiration and understanding, throats and promises. This is the truo foundation of discipline and instruction in morals and in life.[1]

One hundred and twenty years after these lines were written by one of the first ideologists of the Russian aristocracy, Chernyshevsky, one of the first exponents of the Russian proletariat, admonished his readers that, whenever a man behaves badly, we may see in his misdeeds not his fault but his misfortune, if we look carefully into the circumstances of his life. All our enlighteners of the 1860's agreed with Chernyshevsky. His doctrine and that of his adhorents was more humane than that of Kantemir. To be sure, everything its time! It would be strange to find Peter's "nestling" advocating views which menaced "the foundation of the autocratic order." Even in the West at the time of Kantemir such views were only in a state of inception; they were conditioned by the development of social life in the more advanced countries.

In one of his Letters on Nature and Man (namely the fourth one), there is an intelligent representation of what was called later by Moleschott the "Circle of Life" (Kreislauf des Lebens).

---

[1] Kantemir, op. cit., vol. 2, p. 80.

It reads: "Food, being lifeless, animates the beast and becomes itself animal; the former parts disappear insensibly in the continual change. What had for four years been a horse has become dust and ashes, just as what was oats or hay has become the same strong horse."[1] Since "lifeless food" animates the beast, when the oats and hay are converted into a horse, and the horse, in the course of time, becomes "dust and ashes," then it seems that there is no such abyss between the organism having consciousness and the "lifeless substance" as was devised by the dualists. Assuredly, followers of Descartes will tell us that the horse, as well as any other animal, has no consciousness. Such a statement, however, would be meaningless to Kantemir. He declares that "though the animal is not intelligent in many things, it understands much in some matters, and, therefore, we must not think that there is no sense in this creature."[2] How can one reconcile this statement with Kantemir's dualism? Our philosopher evades this difficulty with the help of the hypothesis of a creator. "Every motion that takes away force needs reinforcement, and that is why we find rest in oblivion or in sleep. Who defined this rest and who has determined the time necessary for our tired bodies to repose, etc.?"[3]

1
Ibid., p. 46.
2
Ibid., pp. 48-49. Compare also p. 58.
3
Ibid., p. 46.

138

Substance, or as Kantemir calls it, "hideous substance,"
is inert in itself. Only Divine Will makes it movable. Kantemir
was firmly convinced also that "substance cannot think."[1] He does
admit for a moment that it is possible for substance to think and
again puts forward the argument of "an interval of rest between two
conditions." He says:

> It is necessary that there be some degree of motion in which
> substance has no consciousness; then come other stages when
> substance recognizes itself and begins to reason. Who chose
> the exact degree of their motions? Who found a line in which
> the parts of substance began to move? Who found the exact
> measure, size and figure necessary to every part so as not to
> lose its relation to other parts?[2]

Of course, Kantemir refers to materialism as being un-
worthy of attention. He writes: "All Epicurean philosophers are
so weak and confused that they cannot prove clearly their philosophical position. They acknowledge the atoms as eternal, but do not
explain why. In general, the Epicureans detect the falsehood of
their own principles."[3] Except for the Epicureans, it seems that
he had no idea about other materialists. Even in connection with
the Epicureans, he constantly contradicts himself. In Kantemir's
translation of a letter of Horace, there is a reference to the
Ionian poet Mimnermus: "This poet finds the highest delight in

---

[1] Ibid., p. 58.
[2] Ibid., p. 49.
[3] Ibid., p. 88.

sensuality; 300 years later, the philosopher Epicurus, founder of the Epicurean sect, put this same philosophy on a sound basis."[1]

It is impossible to present a more negative (and a more unfair) criticism of the Epicurean system. Though Horace associated himself with the "Epicurus herd," Kantemir valued him very highly. When Horace, his favorite Latin poet, intimates in his first epistle to Maecenas that to follow Aristippus (whose doctrine he identifies with that of Epicurus) means "to subordinate things to oneself and not oneself to things," Kantemir hastens to remark: "It is true, the best in the philosophy of Aristippus and Epicurus was that we could use everything without subordinating ourselves to anything."[2] He does not observe that such a "science" is very far from the doctrine of "delight in sensuality."

Once more: Kantemir knew very little of the history of philosophy and, therefore, was not always able to judge individual philosophers. Tatishchev's thought was sounder and more logical.[3]

---

[1] Ibid., vol. 1, pp. 434-435. Compare the footnote on p. 394 of the same volume.

[2] Ibid., pp. 394-395.

[3] While in Paris, Kantemir entertained friendly relations with Pierre Louis Moreau de Maupertuis (1698-1759), a writer on philosophical subjects; the latter approached them much more forcefully than Kantemir. (Voltaire was wrong in mocking him.) It is surprising that this association with Maupertuis had so little influence on Kantemir's philosophical conceptions. The relatively slight impression can be explained only by the fact that his mind was scarcely prepared for deep questions. It is true, the major works of Maupertuis were published only after Kantemir's death, but Maupertuis' theories had been known long before they were published.

No matter how weak the arguments put forth by Kantemir in his philosophical letters, they deserve our attention, not only because they are the first philosophical fruits of Europeanized Russian thought, but also because many of those questions which Kantemir tried to solve, even though unsuccessfully, did not cease to interest Russian intellectuals up to the time of Chernyshevsky and Dobrolyubov. Such was, for instance, the problem of the freedom of will and also that of the theoretical foundation of the right to punish. I shall say even more: Chernyshevsky and Dobrolyubov, the most advanced and most noble examples of Russian enlightenment, also discussed materialism at length. Of course, they were acquainted with this philosophy much more thoroughly than Kantemir, and, besides, in contrast to him, they regarded the materialists with undivided sympathy, particularly the leader of the "sect," their contemporary, Feuerbach. This difference in attitude was justified by the circumstances; its explanation constitutes one of the most important problems of my further work.

Later Kantemir was reproached because his moral conceptions lacked preciseness and were eclectic. According to Golakhov, Kantemir made no positive, unequivocal demands for perfect virtue, since the acts of any man which are less than completely virtuous invite scorn. The philosophy of Kantemir is timid and modest, as was his character; it preaches the good, with a fear; it condemns vice, with a blush. Characterizing this moral philosophy, Golakhov comparos it to the Epicurean ethics of Horace, who, as we know,

was among tho most beloved authors of Kantemir. All of Horace's

practical philosophy may be condensed into two or three ideas,

into two or three desires:

> Here is what he wants: peace, moderation and indifference as
> to the "rainy day." Such a philosopher as Horace, of course,
> will not try to improve society's defects: he only laughs at
> them. The tone of his satire is smooth; Kantemir's is the
> same. This accounts for the close similarity between them.

The similarity between them is obvious, but it is only

superficial. In this case, perhaps more than in any other, one

must remember that when two people say the same thing, they do not

necessarily mean the same. The "golden mean" of Horace is the

fruit of social indifference that spread through Rome after the

fall of the republic. It is a decline of morals. The "golden mean"

of Kantemir came from a different source. It did not point to a

decline of the existing social order, but only marked the peculiar

situation of a new social group which appeared as a result of the

reforms of Peter the Great; this group was destined to grow and

forge ahead in spite of many painful obstacles.

"Peter's nestlings" appeared to be the mainstay of the

Russian intelligentsia. After the death of the "Great Reformer,"

with whose reign were linked all the hopes of his "nestlings,"

they found themselves in a very difficult position. During the

reign of Peter the Second their situation seemed almost hopeless.

In his first satire, written in 1729, while he was still twenty,

Kantemir complained bitterly and recalled the period of reformation, as a "golden age." He wrote in verse:

> The time in which wisdom ruled everything and only wisdom dis-
> tributed fame, being alone able to raise us to the highest
> ideals - this period was not to be ours. The "golden age"
> did not reach our generation. Pride, laziness, riches over-
> came wisdom, and science gave way to ignorance. Ignorance
> walks proudly under a bishop's mitre, clad in the richest
> clothes; it tries the people in the judge's room and leads the
> regiments in battle. Science is denuded, abused and driven
> out of all homes; no one wants to know science and all avoid
> friendship....

What was our young enlightener to do in such a cheerless epoch? He could only expect a better future and, while waiting for it, remember that to escape from evil sometimes serves a good purpose. Scornfully Kantemir decided to conform his life to this precept. He writes:

> When you hear such words and see such examples, keep silent,
> my spirit! Do not be discouraged because your talents are not
> recognized! He who hides himself in his quiet corner has a
> life without fear even though it seems to be hard. If Provi-
> dence has given you any understanding, enjoy yourself in your
> privacy. When you explain the sciences to others, do not look
> for praise; you may receive harsh words instead.

These words contain the secret of our author's "golden mean." Russian noblemen of those days had to serve the state; they might enter this compulsory service with varying degrees of ambition. Those aiming at high rank did not have to be particular as to the means they chose. The scrupulous had to be satisfied with "non-eminence"; "not to be bored" with this work was possible, in the words of Kantemir, only for those who were content with little.

Why did Kantemir say that they had to be satisfied with little? In order to keep oneself relatively free. What purpose was such freedom to serve? That one many enjoy "divine wisdom" and study the aims of the sciences. Let us be just and say that only a man of the highest morals could find satisfaction in such pursuits.

Kantemir seriously intended to follow the advice which he gave to his "mind." He himself says that he wrote his first satire only to idle away his time, with no intention of ever publishing it. At that time he felt that he was all alone. He continues:

> By accident one of his friends took the satire with him to read. The latter showed it to Feofan, Bishop of Novgorod, who circulated it everywhere, and, upon returning it, praised it with verses of his own[1] and, as a present, sent him a book: Heraldia of Gods and Poets. Archimandrite Krolik also wrote many verses in praise of the author....[2] Encouraged, Kantemir began to devote himself to writing satires.

Convinced that his writings could arouse general interest, Kantemir abandoned his private contemplations of "divine wisdom," and, according to Prokopovich, started out on that "glorious path travelled by all literary Titans."

---

[1] These are already known to us: "I do not know who you are, a horned prophet..."

[2] The Latin verses: "Ars est celebris stultitiae genus"... See Kantemir, Works, edited by Efremov, vol. 1, pp. 23-24.

Prokopovich was not only as greedy as a wolf and as sly as a fox but had a brilliant mind and a broad cultural background. He knew perfectly well that to follow the above-mentioned path was not easy in the Russia of his period. But he declared that people inspired by Apollo should not fear the opinions of "fools in high places." He wrote:

> Ignore their threats completely; you are thrice fortunate.
> It is good that God gave you a sound mind. Let the whole
> world be angry with you; you are quite happy without favors
> from such fools.

This is excellently expressed. But I shall remind the reader that, during that period, only those who adhered to Kantomir's "golden mean" could really be "happy without happiness."

In Anna's reign the situation of the "Learned Guard" improved somewhat. In spite of this betterment, things were not any too happy. At that time, too, one could reach high ranks only with the aid of plots and intrigues. As was very well said by Chistovich, men of influence of that epoch struck at each other through their seditions and intrigues, expecting a similar treatment for themselves. Let us recollect the spying practices of Prokopovich, the "miraculous high priest." Under such circumstances, the "golden mean" of Kantemir was the only guarantee of some measure of independence.

Kantemir's love of knowledge extended also to politics. His foreign biographer, Abbé Venuti, writes that Kantemir was enthusiastic about the work of Bossuet, Politique sacree. Evidently, this is nothing else but Politique tirée des propres paroles de l'Ecriture Sainte. According to the same biographer:

> The political opinions of the Russian Ambassador were influenced more by the philosophy of the Holy Scripture and by humane interests than by the book of Machiavelli and the intrigues of court life. According to Kantemir, politics should have but one purpose - the welfare of the people. The term "father of the people" is a symbol of the monarch's duties; the interests of the monarch and those of the people must always be the same. The sovereign can buy security and peace, if need be, with the sacrifice of his people, but to spill their blood merely to satisfy his own ambition would violate the laws of nature and of the State.[1]

Kantemir believed that nations are happy only when this rule is the basis of state administration. We know also from the same biographer that Kantemir, meeting a Cabinet minister while both were leaving a theatre, said: "I do not understand how you can bring yourself to attend a theatre right after signing the death sentence of a hundred thousand people." A war had been declared just then.[2] This remark represents a very attractive side of Kantemir.

---

[1] Works, "Introduction" by V. Stoyunin, vol. 1, p. XCVIII.

[2] Ibid., p. XCIX. Apparently the conversation referred to the War of the Spanish Succession. But Cardinal Fleury, who probably signed the decision for France's participation in this War, did not seem to favor it.

What can one say about his enthusiasm for the Politics of Bossuet?
While in Russia, Kantemir became a convinced partisan of absolutism,
as were all other "nestlings of Peter", and, as we shall see later,
he took an active part in the strife of the gentry against the
"nobles by birth" in the latter's attempt to restrict the power of
Empress Anna. When he came to Paris in September, 1738, the local
enlighteners had already begun an energetic campaign against the
ancien régime. The political question had not yet been broached
from a radical point of view. The opposition among progressive
intellectuals, on the other hand, being in sympathy with the English
system of government, was vocal in its demand for civil equality.
Montesquiou wrote from England in 1729: "A Londres, liberté et
égalité" (there is liberty and equality in London). Ten years
later, Marquis D'Argenson urged the necessity of abolishing the
privileges of the nobles. He remarked: "Les nobles ressemblent à
ce que sont les frelons aux ruches" (the nobles resemble drone bees
in a beehive). That this member of our "Learned Guard" did not remain indifferent to what was taking place at that time in progressive
French literary circles is proved by his translation of the Persian
Letters of Montesquiou,[1] issued as early as 1721. Fontenelle, whom
Kantemir also translated, may be considered one of the early pro-

---

[1] The translation has not been preserved.

moters of the literature of enlightenment in France.[1]

We know that Kantemir did not lose his religious beliefs. His devotion to his sovereign seemed to remain unwavering as well: only a partisan of autocratic monarchy could be captivated by the Politics of Bossuet. Nevertheless, it is necessary to make a distinction here. Bossuet was an ideologist of French absolute monarchy and not of Russian tzarism. Therefore, he claimed that there can be no human power higher than the authority of the absolute sovereign and distinguished carefully between an autocratic form of government and an arbitrary one (gouvernement que l'on appelle arbitraire). In this differentiation he agreed entirely with Bodin.

In Bossuet's works, the arbitrary form of government shows the following four characteristics:

First: the subjects are born slaves, that is to say, they are truly slaves. No free man exists among them.[2]

Second: there are no private property rights; everything belongs to the monarch.

Third: the monarch can, at his discretion, dispose of the property of his subjects, as well as of their lives, as is the case with slaves.

Fourth: there is no other law than the will of the monarch.

---

[1]. Lanson says about his book, Histoire des oracles (1687): "Tous les arguments purement philosophiques dont on battra la religion, sont en principe dans le livre de Fontenelle."

[2] Bossuet, Oeuvres complètes, vol. 24, Paris, 1885, pp. 104-105.

Bossuet calls such forms of government barbarous and odious. As such it is foreign to the conceptions of the French and, therefore, has no place in a France ruled by an autocratic monarchy.[1] In the absolute states the subjects maintain their right of property and freedom. Consequently Bossuet calls this form of government a lawful one.[2]

This characterization would be accepted not only by Bodin but by Yury Krijanić as well. It is interesting to note that Bossuet refers to the same biblical story as Krijanić when he describes instances of arbitrary government: the story of how the vineyard of Naboth was appropriated in behalf of the Israelite king, and Naboth himself was beaten with stones because he dared to resent being deprived of the inheritance of his fathers. According to the famous French prelate, God punished Ahab and Jezebel severely because they tried arbitrarily to dispose of the property, honor and life of one of their subjects.[3] We regret that we have no information to show what impression this opinion of Bossuet made on Kantemir, who was acquainted not only with the French "legitimate" monarchy, but also with other forms of monarchy.

---

[1]
Ibid., p. 105.
[2]
Ibid., pp. 105-106.
[3]
Ibid., p. 109. Krijanić thought the same.

When Kantemir declared that the interests of a sovereign
and those of his people must always go hand in hand, he only repeated one of the basic tenets of Bossuet's Politics. The original
reads as follows: "Il n'y a que les ennemis publics qui separent
l'intérêt du prince de l'intérêt de l'Etat" (only the enemies of
society can separate the interests of the monarch from the interests
of the state).[1] Still it does not follow that the Russian satirist
and diplomat gave much thought to the advantages of legitimate
monarchy over the arbitrary one of Russia.

In June, 1732, in answer to a letter of Ostermann, who
demanded from him information concerning the author of an English
article prejudicial to the Russian court, Kantemir wrote: "It is
difficult to know all that is printed in this city every day. I
even dare to say to your Excellency that I do not know if it is
worth looking into the matter, because the people here are free...
and much inclined to talk about what is forbidden..." A few years
later, in a letter to his Empress, he points out again the devotion
of the English to freedom of speech. He says: "Indeed, the English
consider the free press as the foundation of their liberty."[2] But
if Montesquieu, who chanced to be in England, was jealous of English
freedom, it seems that Kantemir remained indifferent to it. In his
correspondence, there is no trace of sympathy for such liberty.

---

[1] Ibid., p. 2.
[2] Kantemir, Works, vol. 2, pp. 97 and 99.

This attitude recalls the indifference of the monks of Moscow toward the liberty of the Lithuanians to change their religion freely. Our monks made reference to this liberty, but they had no desire to practice it at home. The question arises once more: is it possible that our enlightener was like these monks?

The material at our disposal for his biography, which is not always clear, gives us the pleasant opportunity to answer this question negatively. Abbé Venuti writes of Kantemir's "delight with England, where Parliament prescribes the power of the king and does not permit him authority beyond the laws which protect the rights of the subjects against the dire consequences of absolutism."[1]

It is difficult to reconcile Kantemir's enthusiasm for the English constitution and his sympathy for the Politics of Bossuet, the theorist of French absolutism. It is not known how this contradiction was solved in Kantemir's mind. Our satirist told Abbé Venuti that, "as early as 1730, he was able to appreciate the advantages of political liberty but found that, 'under present conditions,' it would be better to preserve the existing political order." This last statement might explain Kantemir's resistance to the efforts of the nobles to limit the absolute powers of

---

[1] V. Stoyunin, "Introduction" to the Works of Kantemir (ed. 1867), p. LVI. Venuti's biography of Kantemir is attached to the French translation of Kantemir's satires. Unfortunately, I could not find this translation in the Bibliothèque Nationale of Paris.

Empress Anna. Such was probably not the case. At that time,
Kantemir, like Prokopovich, was an unconditional partisan of
Russian autocracy, but later, after a sojourn abroad, his eyes
were opened to the advantages of the political institutions of
Western Europe. Eager to calm his conscience, he thereafter resorted to his opportunistic expression of "present conditions."
But, even then, his political views remained vague; he could thus
sympathize both with the absolute monarchy of France and the con-
stitutional system of England. At this time only his dissatisfaction with Russia's autocracy became articulate. Of course, all
this is mere hypothesis. I repeat once more, obscurity abounds here.

Our poor enlightener-diplomat got into tiresome and fruit-
less disputes with foreign writers who criticized Russia's internal
conditions. In the beginning of 1738 he had much trouble with one,
Locatelli, the supposed author of the Lettres Moscovites, which
predicted the early fading of the German party's influence in
Russia. Kantemir wrote to St. Petersburg: "I have tried to learn
from legal experts here if it is possible to arrest and punish the
author of the above-mentioned book." It was impossible to do anything about it, because the liberty of the English forbade retribu-
tive action. Angered by such obstacles or perhaps anxious to ap-
pease the St. Petersburg government, Kantemir assured it that the
English people are continually reminded of the shameless libels
published against the king and his ministers. Not seeing any other

means of punishing Locatelli, he even offered "to take the law in his own hands and to have him beaten up by his secret messengers." If only the Empress would command, Kantemir was ready to carry out this arbitrary means of punishment. At the same time he found it necessary to take further steps to convince himself fully as to the guilt of the supposed author of the Moscow Letters.[1]

Thus, it appears that the difference between legitimate and arbitrary monarchy was not clear to Kantemir. But it is very important for a historian of Russian social thought to know that in acquainting themselves with the political literature of the West, Russians even borrowed some ideas from conservatives like Bossuet, though such ideas were foreign to Russia and must have appeared purely fantastic to her people.

Even though Kantemir preserved his political innocence, one must not think that as a writer he had nothing to say to his contemporaries. Still, because of his education and intellectual development, there was a great difference, almost an abyss, between him and the majority of his readers. We have already become convinced of this difference by reading the footnotes to his translations of foreign authors. This impression is accentuated if we consider very carefully the manifold contents of his satires.

---

[1] Kantemir, op. cit., vol. 2, pp. 101-102.

Kantemir did not consider literature, particularly poetry,
an occupation worthy of a mature man of social rank. Nevertheless,
he was attracted to it, among other things, through a sense of duty
to his country: he hoped, by his literary activity, to be of service
to Russia. Kantemir began to translate the works of Anacreon, probably not without hesitation, since they did not contain any didactic
element. At any rate, he justified himself beforehand by saying:
"Though one would think from Anacreon's songs that he was a drunkard
and a man of easy living, an entirely different opinion was re-
·corded by many ancient writers; therefore, we must suppose that
Anacreon's cheerful disposition was the reason for such writings."[1]
Kantemir enjoyed greatly the Odes of Horace, mainly because of
their moral content. He says about these odes: "Almost every line
contains some rule useful in organizing and improving one's life."[2]
He wrote his own "little works" also because he expected them to
contribute to this "improvement of life." He said: "I write because I consider it my duty as a citizen to do so. I avoid anything
that could bring harm to my fellow-citizens." Prokopovich encouraged Kantemir to follow this attitude in his literary activity:
"While on the glorious path of literary Titans, you began to criticize those who could not appreciate the work of the 'Learned Guard'
and continued to uproot all outworn and harmful customs with the

---

[1]
Ibid., vol. 1, p. 343.
[2]
Ibid., p. 385.

sole purpose of bringing about a happy change in your people..."

The enlighteners of all countries adopted this noble view
in their literary works.[1] Our enlighteners of the 1860's, who devoted themselves with such enthusiasm to literature, Chernyshevsky,
Dobrolyubov, Pisarev, and others, were also eager to offer their
countrymen precepts useful "in organizing and improving one's life."
The contents of these rules differ: Chernyshevsky and Dobrolyubov
did not look at things in the same light as Tatishchev and Kantemir.

The view that literature is not an occupation worthy of
a mature person is not reconcilable with the opinion that it is an
instrument for organizing one's life. Yet Kantemir, as well as
his contemporaries, combined both of these concepts. At first,
this seems unusual. The strangeness disappears if one takes into
consideration that, while adopting the doctrines of the enlighteners
of Western Europe, Kantemir did not cease to be, like Tatishchev,
an apologist for the bureaucratic class. In this capacity, again
like Tatishchev, he could be guided by the above-mentioned doctrines
only to a limited extent. Naturally then, Kantemir is at times
guilty of contradictions, not only in his life and his actions, but
in his ideas as well.

---

[1]
Much was written about this view and the extent to which it dominated the society of the French enlighteners of the 18th century.
I shall mention as one of the recent works, F. Gueff, Le Drame
en France au XVIIIe siècle, Paris, 1910. The third part of this
book deserves special attention; it deals with the different explanations of the effect of enlightening ideas on French belles-
lettres, preeminently on the drama.

CHAPTER III

DIRECT INFLUENCE OF PETER'S REFORM UPON THE DEVELOPMENT

OF RUSSIAN SOCIAL THOUGHT

We know now that the Russians had to pay heavily for
Peter's reform. We have yet to dwell on the opposition of the
people to the new burden imposed by their harsh reformer. The reform, however, was rooted in social necessity, and it was developing slowly but steadily. In fact, the population could not but
observe the good side of the measures. A few outstanding men
early perceived the advantages which the reform would bring to
Russia. Consequently they were in sympathy with it. At times
their enthusiasm was concealed, but at other times it was outspoken
and unbounded. It will suffice to point to the work of Pososhkov
and Lomonosov.

1. IVAN POSOSHKOV[1]

Ivan Pososhkov's Poverty and Wealth is his outstanding
work, and it was published by M. P. Pogodin in 1842. When Pogodin
read the book, he congratulated himself on having "been fortunate

---

[1]
This chapter has been somewhat condensed. Ivan Tikhonovich
Pososhkov (1670-1726) is an interesting figure that belongs both
to the old and the new regime. His most important works are:
The Mirror, Father's Testament and Poverty and Wealth. - Trans-
lator's note.

enough to have discovered a 'Russian genius,' who understood clearly political economy fifty years before its birth in Western Europe, and, in some instances, anticipated Adam Smith."[1] Many investigators, Brikner among them, held a similar high opinion of Pososhkov as an economist. It must be added that some of Pososhkov's practical proposals were considered so bold during the forties of the last century that the book could not be published without the permission of Nicholas I. Later, it became known that Pososhkov had died in the Peter-Paul Fortress, where he had been imprisoned, no doubt, because of the opinions expressed in his book. In view of these circumstances, he acquired a reputation not only as an outstanding theorist but also as an audacious innovator. This was the view of Pavlov-Silvansky, probably the most painstaking scholar of all those who wrote about Pososhkov.

This self-made "orphan of the tzar" built up as much as he tore down. From a scientific viewpoint, however, his theories and practical plans were not as great as Pogodin, Brikner, Miklashevsky and Pavlov-Silvansky would have us believe. All this enhances rather than decreases the significance of his literary activities for the historian of Russian social thought.

---

[1]
Pososhkov, Works, ed. by M. P. Pogodin. Preface to vol. 1, p. VIII, Moscow, 1842. Compare Pogodin's essay in Moscovite, 1842, bk. 3, p. 101.

Pavlov-Silvansky considered Pososhkov a typical Moscow progressive, in contrast with such "Occidentalists" as Peter and his "Learned Guard."[1] What did he mean by the expression "Moscow progressive"? The same critic characterized Pososhkov's credo as that of an orthodox, blended with "extreme superstition."[2] This well-founded opinion is amply demonstrated by such works of Pososhkov's as The Mirror and Father's Testament.

The renowned Bishop Dimitry of Rostov, who had studied thoroughly all differences between the Orthodox Church and the Russian heretics, pronounced Pososhkov's Mirror the "greatest philippic against heretics and a proof of their shame." Bishop Dimitry may have been right; nevertheless, Pososhkov's "good and helpful booklet" is as limited in its outlook as the teachings of the old believers, and, as it is permeated with fanatical intolerance, it could well serve as an arraignment of the old Moscow order. Pososhkov bluntly states that "Patriarch Nicon did well to command the faithful to have nothing to do with the heretics."[3] Addressing the members of the ruling Church, Pososhkov tells them to bear in mind that St. John, the silver-tongued, "prohibits friendship with the enemies of the Church; if any one eats or drinks or in any way

---

[1] Essay "I. T. Pososhkov" in N. P. Pavlov-Silvansky's Works, vol. 2, p. 61.

[2] Ibid., p. 54.

[3] Pososhkov, Works, Moscow, 1863, vol. 2, p. 233.

communicates with heretics, he shall suffer even more than the
enemies of the Church themselves. Stay away from false teachers
or prophets; they are enemies of Christ and friends of the Antichrist. All these false prophets and atheists are children of
Satan and his son, "the Antichrist."[1]

The same spirit pervades Pososhkov's Father's Testament:
"Do not hesitate, my son, to destroy the enemies of God - the
heretics; God Himself ordered you to fell and to burn down a fruit-
less tree." The "Moscow progressive" does not confine himself to
his plea of burning heretics. He finds fierce words for the expression of such barbaric advice. "If any bones of the burnt remain, you must grind them up and burn them once more; you must then
mix the ashes with excrement and cast them all into inaccessible
swamps, so that none of their followers may gather the ashes and
make of them a sacred relic."[2]

The reader sees how very far removed Pososhkov was from
the religious tolerance advocated, at least in theory, by the
"Occidentalist" Vasily Tatishchev. Pososhkov was not by nature a
cruel man. He advised his son to be gentle and kind, not only to
human beings, but to animals as well - "even a hen is a creation

[1]
Ibid., p. 236.
[2]
Father's Testament, op. cit., published by E. M. Prilejaev,
St. Petersburg, 1893, pp. 194-195, 280, 295.

of God...." He goes still further and advises him, wherever possible, to spare the life of plants. "In the woods, take care that you do not fell any tree unless it is absolutely necessary. God has planted trees for the benefit of mankind and not as things to play with or to destroy."[1] Under other circumstances, Pososhkov might well have come to a true recognition of his close relationship with all things in nature and might have formulated rules of conduct in accordance with his inner beliefs, but in the Moscow of his time the author of The Mirror and The Father's Testament emerged.

It is easy to guess that Pososhkov was a monarchist, for there were no republicans in the Russia of that day, but it is hard to understand how deeply his views - and not only his political ones - were steeped in the spirit of feudal monarchy. "Foreign kings have less power than their subjects, especially the merchants," wrote Pososhkov, but he added that in Russia everything was different. "All power belongs to our absolute monarch and not to aristocrats or democrats... The tzar is the lord of his empire just as God is the Lord of all creation."[2] An economic law is deduced from this political theory: the tzar can determine at will the value of the Russian currency.

---

[1] Ibid., pp. 13-14.
[2] Pososhkov, Works, op. cit., vol. 1, pp. 73-74, 231, 254.

We see how erroneous was the opinion of our scholars that Pososhkov was a profound theorist and anticipated certain discoveries of Western European economists. Ideas grow hand in hand with the development of material goods. Since the government of Moscow was less advanced than other European states in the field of economics, it is only natural that Russia's "first economist" should have been far behind his European colleagues. In France, where social and political thought had developed for centuries in the direction of absolutism, the publicists were more and more inclined to recognize the right of the ruler to interfere in all phases of national existence. But European monarchy was not of the "patriarchal" type; because of this, French theorists such as Bodin and Bossuet differed radically from Moscow thinkers.

In the field of economics 14th century France already had writers who better understood the value of money than did Pososhkov at the end of the 17th century. France could boast of Buridan and Nicolas Oresme[1] in the 14th century. It was Buridan who stated that a king does not have the right to decree the market value of money, although he can change, in an emergency, the weight and denomination of a current coin. His pupil, Nicolas Oresme, expressed himself even more definitely against the monarch's power

---

[1] Oresme, N. Died 1382. Works: De Origine, natura, jure et mutationibus monetarum, translated by Plekhanov into French as: Traité de l'invention des monnaies.

to evaluate money. According to Oresme, money is not the king's private property; it belongs to the whole nation. To change the value of an established coin arbitrarily means to violate the rights of all the people. Encroachments on the people's rights are crimes, and such criminal acts are detrimental not only to the nation, but to the king as well. Pososhkov could never have entertained such an idea. Oresme believed that the king's undue interference with the monetary system would undermine his authority, because "the great French kings had never resorted to tyranny, and Frenchmen were unaccustomed to slavish submission, so that if a king tried to deviate from this policy, he was likely to lose his throne." Such ideas could never have entered Pososhkov's mind because he was not a native and thinker of the French kingdom but lived in Russia's patriarchal monarchy.

Pososhkov condemns the methods of western merchants in Russia. These merchants take advantage of their position in the nation, he claimed. "They determine the value of their goods in terms of money and invoke the person of the ruler as proof that the value they set on their stock is correct." Russia is not Europe, and "according to our simple way of thinking, such a situation would bring dishonor to the good name of the ruler, because money would then derive its strength not from his name imprinted on the coin, as should be the case, but from its commercial value." In view of this "simple way of thinking," we can hardly expect from Pososhkov any discoveries in the field of economic theory.

It was Ganilh who stated correctly that Italy was always the country with the worst currency and the best treatises on money. If in the 14th century Italy did not have economists like Oresme, she could at least boast of Diomedes Carafa, a century later. His De regis et boni principis officio[1] is founded on the theory that a king is as rich as his subjects: "Subditorum facultates potentiae regiae fundamentum existimari oportet." Pososhkov began to develop the same theory in the beginning of the 18th century. Carafa also insisted that justice was necessary for the economic welfare of a state: "Ubi aequum vigeat imperium, ibi florere urbes; contra ubi vi agatur, ibi omnia in deterius ruere ac celeriter evanescere." Pososhkov expressed the same idea in his book on Poverty and Wealth, but this book was finished in 1724, two hundred and thirty-seven years after the death of Carafa.

Sixteenth century Italy produced two brilliant economists, Gaspare Scaraffi and Bernardo Davanzati. In 1579, Count Scaraffi wrote a most important book, Discorso sopra le monete e della vera proporzione fra l'oro e l'argento; it was published in 1582. He introduced the concept of a universal unit of money, a unit to be used by all civilized states (zecca universale). The famous work

---

[1] See: J. Rico-Salerno, Storia delle dottrine finanziarie in Italia, Palermo, 1896, pp. 47-56.

of Antonio Serra was published in 1613. His Breve Trattato delle
cause che possono far abbondare i regni d'oro e d'argento gave Italians
the opportunity of calling Antonio Serra "the founder of political
economy."[1] This is without doubt an exaggeration. But, surely,
this Italian economist of the 17th century could have learned nothing
from Pososhkov.

Finally, if we compare the economic theories contained in
Poverty and Wealth with the opinions of such English writers as
William Petty and Dudley North, we shall again see to what extent
the development of social ideas depends on the development of
material goods. England had far surpassed Russia in the field of
industry and commerce. In the 17th century, Britain had economists
able to discuss and solve correctly the most important problems of
business and finance - problems whose existence Pososhkov did not
and could not suspect (among them, the exchange value of goods).

Pavlov-Silvansky gives Pososhkov credit for the notion
that the true wealth of a nation lies not in the abundance of gold
in its treasury, but in the welfare of the population.[2] In the first

---

1
   Giuseppe Pecchio, Storia della economia publica in Italia, Torino,
   1852, p. 52.

2
   Pavlov-Silvansky, following A. Miklashevsky, maintains that Pososhkov's work is more valuable than the writings of the German mercantilists both in language and thought content. But the economic
   literature of contemporary Germany was so retarded, that it is
   better to omit it and to refer to the literatures of France, Italy
   and England.

place, this idea was expressed in Russia before him by Yury Krijanic, and secondly, even Krijanić was not its originator. The thought was quite current in Western Europe long before Krijanić's time. I can mention two exponents of this idea in the 15th century: John Fortescue and D. Carafa. In 1613 Montchrétien wrote in his <u>Traité d'economie politique</u>: "<u>La richesse de vos sujets est vôtre</u>." Vauban wrote that the king is to the state what the head is to the body; a king, therefore, should see to it that the revenues and taxes imposed on the people do not deprive them of their means of existence.[1] Boisguillebert expressed the same opinion in his work, <u>Le Détail de la France</u> (1695) and in <u>Factum de la France</u> (1706): "<u>La richesse des sujets est l'unique base de la richesse des princes.</u>"

This idea was clear to Vauban, Boisguillebert and many other economists, and assuredly none of them ever went so far as to maintain that the working population of a state is the property of the king in the same sense as the feudal lord of the Middle Ages had control over his serfs. A statement from them to this effect would have been meaningless, because the very notion was foreign to European social and political institutions. Vauban plainly asserts that a state could not continue to exist (and sustain itself) if its subjects refused to maintain it, and, in order to be able to support the state, the people require some kind of capital.

---

[1] Vauban, <u>La dixme royale</u>, published in 1707, but written not later than 1699.

When Pososhkov stated that the welfare of the peasants was the welfare of the tzar, he hastened to add that the peasants were the property of the tzar. He said: "The landowners are not the permanent owners of their peasants; that is why the landowners do nothing to help the peasants. The tzar of all Russia is the sole owner of the peasants."[1] This statement of Pososhkov's is correct, indeed, and corresponds with the social structure of Moscow's patriarchal monarchy. He added that the peasants should be guided and guarded by the ukases of the tzar, in order that they may "remain peasants, rather than become paupers."[2]

This also was in accordance with the spirit of the old Moscow order. Kotoshichin once wrote:

> Estates and patrimonies are given to noblemen and to persons of rank; the owners, by virtue of their grants, can tax the peasants and collect from them as much as possible, but taxes must be levied within reason in order to keep the peasants on the estate, and not to make paupers of them.

This meant an infringement of the tzar's interests. If we believe Kotoshichin, estates and patrimonies were taken away from the "exploiters" and handed over to their relatives of good behavior.[3] We do not know how often exploiters were thus punished, but these cases must have been rare. Still Pososhkov had an ox-

---

[1] Pososhkov, Works, op. cit., vol. 1, p. 183.

[2] Ibid., p. 183.

[3] G. Kotoshichin, Russia in the Time of Alexis Michailevich, vol. 1, p. 237.

cellent knowledge of Moscow life, and he must have known that in
the reign of Peter's father the government had given some signs of
solicitude for the peasants. He must also have understood that
this interest was nothing more than one for the government treasury.
Thus Pososhkov's political credo was nothing startling and his proposal to Peter that he limit the exploitation of the peasants by
the boyars was nothing new. His scheme fitted perfectly into the
spirit of Moscow's practice; that is why, when he proposed his
plan, he hastened to add that the welfare of the peasants was the
welfare of the tzar.

The government punished "exploiters" only if they harmed
the interests of the state too flagrantly. It must not be forgotten,
however, that economic theories had little to do with this procedure.
According to old Russian practice, punishment was exercised by the
bureaucracy. Since those very exploiters of the peasants were
often the same bureaucrats who, in the interests of the treasury,
adopted measures for the protection of the peasants from exploitation, it is not at all surprising that these measures were neither
forceful nor adequate.

Pososhkov was, of course, not a bureaucrat, but a "tzar's
orphan" (taxpayer) by birth and a merchant by class. That is why
he could ask for more decisive action, and in some cases, when
Moscow practice limited itself to vague threats seldom executed,
he demanded definite legislation. Pososhkov proposed the "opening

of a state tax list." The schedule should lay down the amounts of taxes; "a peasant should then be able to pay his tax and still have enough left for his own use and not remain in everlasting want."[1] The courts should supervise the enforcement of the laws, and no landlord should be able to collect over a "definite amount." The owner should have the right to supervise the behavior of his peasants "so that the loafers be segregated and the rest of the peasants may work for their maintenance constantly and diligently. A too lazy peasant should be punished severely, not only by a government official or the landlord, but even by his immediate foreman."[2]

To punish the peasant severely! Indeed, if Pososhkov had really been interested in defending the economic interests of the peasant, it would undoubtedly have occurred to him that it was also necessary to protect the "hide" of the peasant against thrashings.

Pososhkov opposed the system of taxing "souls"; he considered "the soul" to be an abstract and incomprehensible thing, lacking any intrinsic value, and he believed that "only things fixed to the ground, property that is immovable, should be taxed." Since the only immovable thing in the villages was the land, this should be the basis of a new system of taxation: "Common sense

---

[1] Pososhkov, Works, op. cit., vol. 1, p. 183.
[2] Ibid., p. 185.

dictates that the peasant's 'plot' ought to be taxed equitably... in proportion to the amount of land he possesses and the area he cultivates."[1]

In order to evaluate fully Pososhkov's proposal, we must bear in mind that the land tax preceded the head tax in Russia. This situation gave rise to many abuses vividly criticized by our author. The number of "plots" was estimated by the number of gates. Many a boyar continued to register several families under one "plot," and made several "plot" owners use a single gate.[2] "The revenue officers allow but one gate to a plot; regardless of the number of dwellings on it. The boyars' practice of avoiding taxes is most unjust and will bring ruin to the poor peasants."[3]

This was the real reason for Pososhkov's proposal to levy the tax according to the land value. Lappo-Danilevsky asserts, and rightly, that an economic basis of taxing peasants' "plots," that is, according to the size of the field under cultivation, would be tantamount to equalizing land ownership.[4] It seems that Pososhkov realized this, at least so it seems in his Poverty and Wealth: "In my opinion, if a peasant has a whole plot, it is necessary to give

---

[1] Ibid., pp. 186-187.

[2] Ibid., p. 186.

[3] Ibid., p. 186.

[4] Lappo-Danilevsky, Organization of Direct Taxes in Moscow, p. 200.

him enough land for cultivation, that he may sow yearly, for his
own use, four quarts of rye and eight quarts of summer wheat and
harvest twenty bales of hay."[1] It would have been necessary to
resurvey the land in order to realize this scheme.

Pososhkov was the first Russian writer to propose this
practical plan of equalization. French Utopian Socialists supplied
the theoretical foundation for this tangible suggestion, and Russian
publicists of the 19th century gave it a place of honor in their
programs after enlarging considerably on the idea. But Pososhkov
never developed this plan further; he was readily satisfied with
the progressive evolution of the principle of taxation of "plots"
according to their cultivated land. He wrote:

> In case a peasant has so small a tract of land that he is un-
> able to plant even a quart of rye, the revenue collectors
> should be forbidden to place such property on the tax list
> as a whole plot; they must rather assess it only as one sixth
> of a plot.[2]

This may mean equalization of the tax burden, but in no
way is it equitable apportionment of parcels of land. Pososhkov
recommended a general survey and even a cadaster system of land
registry.

In all this we see Pososhkov's understanding and deep
knowledge of contemporary Russian life. He did not, however, overlook those features of the old Moscow system which were beneficial

---

[1]
Pososhkov, _Works, op. cit._, vol. 1, p. 187.
[2]
Ibid., p. 187.

to the lower classes; he advised that they be kept and, if possible,
expanded. It is not surprising that many members of the upper
classes were filled with fear when Pogodin first published <u>Poverty</u>
<u>and</u> <u>Wealth</u> in the 1840's, at a time when the Russian serfs had even
less freedom than in Pososhkov's day. Despite his advanced ideas,
Pososhkov does not deserve the title of a "bold innovator"; if we
must call him a "progressive," let us style him a "Moscow progressive,"
in other words, a man who looked to the past and not to the future,
even when he presented certain demands progressive in the sense
that they were to benefit the people. We know that in his time
there were many such progressives. The fact that our social and
political conditions were still in a period of transition explains
this phenomenon.

Pososhkov's advice to his son on behavior in church shows
the extent to which he was steeped in the spirit of old Moscow. He
pictured the kingdom of God as an Oriental despotic state: "Do not
honor the icons equally, but pay homage and light a larger candle
before the Lord's icon; smaller candles will suffice for His servants."
Even the bows of worship should be graded; the icons should be
kissed in the order of heaven's hierarchy: "Touch your lips to the
foot of Jesus but kiss the hands of the rest of the saints, not
their feet."[1]

1

Pososhkov, <u>Father's</u> <u>Testament</u>, <u>op</u>. <u>cit</u>., pp. 89-90.

Matveev, a contemporary of Pososhkov, stated that in the
rest of Europe children "are brought up by kindness rather than by
blows."[1] This author had felt the softening influence of Western
European ways, whereas Pososhkov, as a "Moscow progressive," thought
along the line of old Moscow tradition. He insisted that the "saints,
in order to save humanity from damnation, had ordered that children
be thrashed without mercy."[2] Pososhkov accepts without criticism
the "all-wise" pedagogic rules given in the Teachings of Jesus Ben
Sirach[3] and he even adds some cruel suggestions of his own to them.
He considered it a sin and an "unpardonable" weakness for a father
to caress his children. Instead he advised that "children be kept
under surveillance and constant fear," adding that "a child should
first be afraid of God; second, he should be fearful of you. They
will grow up to be good people if they are so trained. Otherwise
they will be spoiled by caresses and other indulgences, and they

---

[1]
Sovremennik (Contemporary), 1856, vol. 57, p. 25.
[2]
Pososhkov, Father's Testament, op. cit., p. 44.
[3]
    "Cocker thy son and he will terrify thee;
    Play with him and he will grieve thee.
    Laugh not with him, lest he vex thee
    And make thee gnash thy teeth at the last.
    Let him not have freedom in his youth,
    And overlook not his mischievous acts.
    Bow down his neck in his youth
    And smite his loins sore while he is little -
    Lest he become stubborn and rebel against thee,
    And thou experience anguish of soul on his account."
Bible, Apocryphal Books, Sirach (Chapter 30, lines 9-12).

will enter upon evil ways: they will become drunkards, degenerates or even thieves."[1] Pososhkov is certain that many Russians go under because "they are either schooled insufficiently or are spoiled by indulgent parents."

If his monetary theory demonstrates the naïveté of his economic conceptions, his attempt to brand as a crime the indulgences usually allowed children by their parents shows that his understanding of sociological truths is no less naïve. Of course, sociology as a science was nonexistent in the time of Pososhkov. Nevertheless, there are passages in the Bible which show that crimes are caused by other factors than "overindulgence" shown to childhood. Luther, of whom Pososhkov speaks with such bitter contempt, had a far broader outlook on the causes of crime.[2]

I can also refer to Thomas More's Utopia, where the causes of crime are, on the whole, correctly stated. But Pososhkov remembered only those passages in the Bible which recorded his old-Moscow conceptions of social relationships; too much emphasis was given, in these views, to sticks, whips and even the hangman's rope as means of keeping people on the path of virtue.

---

[1] Pososhkov, Father's Testament, op. cit., p. 43.

[2] "When one is getting along well, he does not fear God... When things become bad, however, flesh and blood can no longer endure bad days... Then it is that man turns to the Lord God."

This characterization of Pososhkov's opinions would not be complete without mentioning his profound dislike for foreigners. Even in his Note on the Conduct of the Army, written after the defeat of the Russian army at Narva and presented to Golovin in 1701, he stated:

> I am greatly surprised, Sir, and quite perplexed that the German people, in spite of their reputation for wisdom and truth, should teach us falsehood. It is very dangerous to believe them; they are not the sincere well-wishers they pretend to be and therefore are not to be trusted. They defraud us in all their transactions with us; they take us for plain fools.[1]

The Father's Testament contains the same distrust of and protest against foreigners: "We cannot consult the Germans on any matter; they cheat us and swindle us out of our money; they will never tell us the truth."[2]

Pososhkov writes with the same distrust of foreigners in Poverty and Wealth. In other words, during his whole life he was consciously distrustful of and hostile to all foreigners.

Pososhkov was born in the village of Pokrovskaye, a suburb of Moscow, which later became a part of the capital. Because of its proximity to the capital, many of those living in Pokrovskaye were peasant-farmers (krestyane) in name only; they earned their living by working in the tzar's summer palace, in Moscow or in

---

[1] Pososhkov, Works, op. cit., vol. 1, pp. 272-273.
[2] Pososhkov, Father's Testament, op. cit., p. 47.

the palace of the Governor. Pokrovskaye was known to the State
Engineering Bureau ever since 1680. During Pososhkov's childhood,
the palace work shops were completely reorganized and enlarged
under the direction of foreign experts. As a child, young Ivan,
while accompanying his father to his work in the Kremlin, would
run in and out of these shops admiring the curious doings of the
craftsmen. He enjoyed watching these men at work in their crafts.
He called them "the arts"; later he got to know a few of these
"arts" himself.

In Pososhkov's works, we notice his intense eagerness to
promote and develop Russia's productive forces and his admiration
for the technical sciences. This was, without doubt, the fruit of
the impressions he received as a child in the palace shops. His
condemnation of laziness has, unquestionably, the same origin: he
observed that Western Europeans knew the value of time. But how
could the productive forces of Russia be developed? How could the
people be made more industrious? Foreigners had to be copied, no
matter how one felt about them. In spite of his own distrust of
the outsider, Pososhkov recommended that foreign masters be received cordially. He wrote in his <u>Poverty</u> and <u>Wealth</u>:

> If some foreign artist or craftsman should visit Russia, he
> should be given a house to live in, and ten or more students
> should be sent to him that they may learn the essentials of
> his art. A contract should be made, and if his teaching is
> conscientious and truthful, he should be paid not only the
> agreed salary but also a bonus for his sincerity and efficiency.

He should be sent off with honors so that other artists and tradesmen may visit Russia and teach our people the different crafts.[1]

As Peter had the same end in view, our author could not but sympathize with his program. The economic system of the Moscow government, however, did not teach the people the significance of the technical sciences or the great value of time. Muscovites entered foreign schools without enthusiasm; therefore Peter found it necessary "to make them study." The same purpose is expressed by Pososhkov when he writes that "without compulsion" it is impossible to bring about results.

But Peter was the tzar and Pososhkov only a "tzar's orphan." As an "orphan" he knew very well the many obstacles that confronted an ordinary Russian who was sent to study with foreigners. It is not surprising that in his Poverty and Wealth, in spite of advising the invitation of foreign masters to Russia, he should complain bitterly about the ill-treatment of "our own artists" by the authorities:

> Although our own Russian administrators do not value the Russian worker and artist highly and thus neglect their care, nevertheless, in the interest of the nation, these people must be fed well enough so that they will not be tempted to steal and lie, and finally, hate their work.[2]

1
Pososhkov, Works, op. cit., vol. 1, p. 145.
2
Ibid., p. 145.

The observation that the authorities had no respect for the Russian people in general and the Russian taxpayers in particular was no doubt made when Pososhkov, while still a young man, visited the state shops supervised by foreigners. It goes without saying that this observation was incompatible with any affection on his part for foreigners, especially since the latter treated the "tzar's orphans" rather roughly.

In the first part of this work, I have mentioned that the turn to the West of the Moscow government was accompanied by widespread hatred of foreigners among the major part of the population. Pososhkov's writings are evidence of this remark. He understood that it was necessary to learn from foreigners, though he noticed that they did not have much sympathy for the Russians and exploited them whenever they had the chance. Therefore, the higher he praised the education of the foreigners, the more he disliked them and the less he trusted them. In Poverty and Wealth we read the following discussion of trade policies:

> The Germans will never teach us thrift; they only glorify those things by which they themselves, and not we, will benefit. They seek profits not only for themselves but for all their fellow Germans. They are trying to ruin us completely; that is why we must know them and also understand something of their commercial, military and technical affairs. Since there is not a word of truth in what they say, we should observe their actions, not their words, and keep them under constant surveillance.[1]

---

[1] Ibid., pp. 126-127; see also p. 212.

As his last and strongest point against the Germans,
Pososhkov refers to their adherence to the teachings of Luther,
whom he called an "archheretic." He assures his son that "Martin
Luther allowed everything to his pupils and granted them universal
indulgence," that is, that he was a prophet of vice.[1] It is almost impossible to find any sin that was not ascribed by Pososhkov
to Martin Luther - "the completely bad and lewd unfrocked priest."
Those attacks of Pososhkov's on the Lutheran faith have special
significance because the "nestlings of Peter" were far more friendly
toward the Protestants than toward the Catholics. These "nestlings,"
however, suffered less from the troubles confronting Pososhkov all
his life. The "Lutherans" made the Russians and, above all, the
common people the objects of their economic exploitation. That "they
did not consider it a sin to swindle these people out of their
money" is especially repugnant to Pososhkov. He disliked them to
such a degree that he expressed preference for Tartars, although
they were of the Mohammedan faith. "Lutherans are worse than cattle,
because at least the cattle know the hand that feeds them; they
are like wolves: chassez le naturel et il revient au galop." It
is known that the Catholics were bent on exploiting the Russians
no less than the Protestants, but the latter occupied positions of

---

[1]
Pososhkov, Father's Testament, op. cit., p. 124.

greater importance and constituted the majority of the foreigners who swept into Russia at the time of the reform and even immediately before it. For this reason Pososhkov confines his attack to the "Lutherans" and forgets the existence of the "Romans" altogether.

In his attacks, Pososhkov reasons from the point of view of the Russian merchant rather than that of the peasant, although he had once identified himself with the peasant class. Of course, he was never a farmer; he occupied himself with many "arts" and at the same time often headed several commercial and manufacturing enterprises. He owned a house in St. Petersburg and two "plots" in Novgorod. By 1718, he became a landowner; he bought the village of Matveeva and also half of Sacarasenie village. In 1724, he purchased a few parcels of land from a nobleman named Unsky. As we see, Pososhkov was not so pitifully poor as he pretended. Although he advised Peter to limit taxes on the peasants, we cannot find that he himself had much sympathy for them. Pososhkov was certain that the main cause of the peasant's plight was his laziness. Of course, our merchant could not very well be sincerely sympathetic with the serfs, especially since he was confronted with the problem of the runaway serf.

His complete and sincere sympathy went to his own merchant class: "The army is responsible for the expansion of tzardom and the merchants for its glorification." We must therefore see in

Pososhkov an ideologist of the commercial and industrial and not of the peasant class. He complained that the exploitation of Russians by foreigners was rooted in the latter's influence in Russia's commercial and business activities. This is easy enough to understand. In advocating that the "window to Europe" be shut, Pososhkov said: "Foreigners trade with such shrewdness that the Russians, naïve in these matters, can scarcely safeguard their interests." In Poverty and Wealth, he shows resentment towards those foreign merchants who bring their bric-a-brac to Russia and sell it at double or triple their actual worth; at the same time they underestimate the value of the basic products of Russia. In order to reverse this process - and this was Pososhkov's main concern - he formulated plans which he submitted to Peter. Indeed, in expressing sympathy with Peter's reform, Pososhkov expressed sympathy for the tzar who took to heart the interests of the merchant class. Before Peter's time, foreigners had followed the custom of bringing presents to the "boyars"; these foreigners were able, by spending only a few hundred rubles, to amass huge profits. "The boyars had a very low opinion of the merchants," wrote Pososhkov; "they would have exchanged all of Russia's tradesmen for the price of a half-penny. Fortunately these days are no more."[1] Peter had seen to it that the foreigners were stopped from buying protection from the boyars, to the detriment and exploitation of the Russian people.

---

[1]
Pososhkov, Works, op. cit., vol. 1, p. 122.

We have now before us one of the countless conditions in which antagonism between the "tzar's servants" and the "tzar's orphans" proved useful to the central power. The "orphans" hoped that their own situation would be improved thereby. We can well understand why the narrow-minded nationalist Pososhkov sympathized with the reform, which actually worked against the interests of the majority of the Moscow nationalists. Pososhkov reverted to the notion that the value of money in Russia should be determined by the will of the tzar: "All authority in Russia is vested in the tzar; only his grace grants us the limited power now in our possession."[1] The taxpayers favored absolute authority for the tzar because they hoped to receive some part of that power as a weapon in their bitter struggle with the bureaucrats (the "tzar's servants").

Still, this was not the only reason why Pososhkov liked Peter. Pososhkov was about twenty years older than Peter. He was already a mature man with definite opinions and a well worked-out philosophy of life when Peter began his reforms. Despite his predominantly conservative opinions, Pososhkov began to realize the evils of the prevailing order. We can see this change - most important to us - from his very odd work, Report on the Correction of All Ills, written before 1704:

---

[1]
Ibid., p. 123.

If some one carefully observed our way of living, he could not
detect a scintilla of common sense in our conduct of affairs;
he would find order neither in our religious institutions,
nor in our literary and artistic pursuits, nor in commerce and
in national affairs... I find nothing that is not defective.
Foreigners mock at our way of living on every occasion.

When a man has come to the sad conviction that everything
is "rotten and unjust" in his country, these two questions come
naturally to his mind: Can the situation be improved? Is the
situation altogether hopeless? Pososhkov was confident that everything could be improved. He insisted:

By renewing our faith we can improve the condition of our
country. We can rectify all the abuses of our civic and
military affairs and implant truth into our spiritual lives,
so that all the world will marvel at us.[1]

The contempt of the foreigners for the Russians aroused
Pososhkov's antagonism. At the same time, it awakened in him a
feeling of national pride, a quality entirely different from the
primitive conceit of the native Muscovites. The opinion that everything is bad at home whereas abroad the people are much better off
left little room for conceit; it rather indicated the desire to
see the Russians reach and even surpass the achievements of foreign
countries. "The Germans are much better informed than we; but, by
the grace of God, we possess a keener power of observation, and we
are not less intelligent than they. Thus it is for naught that
they try to insult us." Pososhkov wrote the above in his Note on

---

[1]
Pososhkov's "Report" reprinted in the Works of Pavlov-Silvansky,
vol. 2, pp. 77-79.

the Conduct of the Army.

His persistence in discussing desired reforms is characteristic of our "Moscow progressive." He believed that Russia was in
great need of reforms which would place religion on a firm foundation. His frequent contacts with foreigners made it clear to him
that the Muscovites could not hope to defend their Orthodox Church
with the religious weapons at their command. "How are we expected
to combat heresies, when we have not even been taught to answer
such questions on religion as a little child might ask?" Study
was, therefore, the essential thing, and, to defend the faith, the
Russians should learn those things which would shed light on religious questions. Accordingly, Pososhkov gives this advice to his
son in the early part of his Testament: "Throughout your school
years, my son, give special attention to languages, not only to
Slavonic, but to Greek and Latin as well; also to Polish, because
many books are published in that language, especially on the
sciences, in which the Poles surpass us." Peter and his "nestlings"
realized that the German language was more important for the Russians
than Polish and the classical languages; but they judged from a
cultural point of view, whereas Pososhkov considered a program of
studies for a Greek-Latin-Slavonic Academy, since he believed into be
telligent defense of the Orthodox faith of primary importance.

The foreigners showed their superiority over the Russians
in other things than disputes over questions of faith. In November,

1700, Charles XII crushed the Russian army near Narva. As we have
remarked above, the disastrous effect of this defeat made a strong
impression on Pososhkov. His remedy for such casualties was included in his Report on the Correction of All Ills. Russia's
military defects were further criticized in his Note on the Conduct
of the Army, written in 1701, in other words, after the Battle of
Narva. Pososhkov complained that our army had been defeated even
in battles where it outnumbered the enemy: "I really cannot understand how we can be proud of our many regiments when they are beaten
by smaller armies and even captured by them."[1] Deeply distrustful
of the foreigners as he was, Pososhkov naturally blamed those out-
siders who had been teaching military science to the Russians.
Closely bound up with this thought was his advice to shut the "window
to Europe" carved out by alien plotters: "We Russians have hands
like the foreigners; these aliens are not gods descending from some
heaven, but mere mortals such as we are. Once we have the desire
and urge, we can accomplish anything."[2]

Pososhkov observed that the Russian soldier was inexperi-
enced in target practice. He remarked shrewdly: "In my opinion,
shooting in mass formation, though interesting to watch, is in-
effective, whereas sharpshooting, while not impressive, will take

---

1
Pososhkov, Works, op. cit., vol. 1, p. 278.
2
Ibid., p. 282.

better effect on the enemy."[1] About one-hundred and fifty years later, one of our military authorities tried to explain this theory: "Contrary to the opinions of the best military tacticians of his time, Pososhkov opposed the machine-like behavior of military units in mass formation. He was in favor of educating the soldier individually; a principle that we, like the rest of Europe, have only recently begun to accept."[2]

How and where Pososhkov, the merchant, acquired a better insight into military matters than specialists is immaterial here. We must, however, keep one thing in mind: in order to fire on the enemy effectively, an army should have good rifles; to make good rifles, we must know "the art of gunmaking," an art in which the foreigners were much better versed than the Russians. Although Pososhkov's xenophobia is well known, he did welcome "craftsmen" from other lands. He advised the hiring of foreign masters, no matter what the cost.[3]

Apparently it was impossible to improve the situation without the aid of the foreigner. Yet, in his Note on the Conduct of the Army, Pososhkov stated that inviting foreign masters was not sufficient to solve the problem. The defense of Russia against

---

[1] Ibid., p. 267.

[2] Military Almanach, 1850, No. 4, p. 365. (Quoted by E. M. Prilojaev in his preface to Pososhkov's Father's Testament, p. XLV.)

[3] Pososhkov, Works, op. cit., vol. 1, p. 269.

invasion was the responsibility of the "tzar's servants"; many cavalry regiments were recruited from their ranks. The defects of these forces were clearly known to the noblemen as early as the 17th century, but the boyars had their own reasons for overlooking the inadequate service of their "brethren." Pososhkov had no such reasons. He never ceased to reiterate the opinion that the noblemen carried out their military duties badly.[1] Poverty and Wealth contains passages against the bureaucracy and the "red tape" of the Moscow administration. Although Pososhkov was in sympathy with the old Muscovite concepts, he supported those of Peter's reforms which abolished the old system of military service. A soldier cannot be good without a thorough military education, to the rigors of which noblemen were not accustomed. Who had promulgated such demands? In the old social and political system of Moscow only a representative of the central administration was empowered to do this. Pososhkov stated this idea in plain words: "For the correction of all prevailing evils only one thing is necessary - the will and desire of a great tzar." The more Peter the Great asserted his will, the more our merchant was in favor of his reforms.

The nobles were not only defenders of Russia but they also ruled the land. Pososhkov realized that they made bad defenders and even worse rulers. He spoke from personal experience when he wrote:

---

[1]
 Ibid., p. 287.

Last year (1719) I wrote to Prince Dimitry Michailevich Golitzin and applied for a license to operate a brewery and sell vodka. As a result, I was arrested without any explanation and was kept in jail for a whole week. I felt lonely and sad because I could not understand why I had been arrested and imprisoned.[1]

Any one would feel despondent in such circumstances! The same arbitrariness brought him his freedom. Pososhkov had begged a prison official to say a few words in his behalf to Prince Golitzin and lo! he was immediately set free; of course, no explanation of his arrest was given nor a guarantee of protection from similar occurrences.

In 1721, Captain Nevelsky sequestered all of Pososhkov's possessions and put him out of his own house. In the same year, Colonel Poretskoy insulted our economist and swore "to set him on his sabre." Pososhkov's appeal to the civil court proved of no avail, because Poretskoy refused to recognize any other authority than that of a military court. In view of such treatment of members of the merchant class, one can well imagine what liberties the nobles allowed themselves toward their peasants. The nobles treated clergymen just as abominably; Pososhkov gives several instances in his writings. In short, all those who were not members of their own class fared badly at the hands of the "tzar's servants."

It is not surprising that Pososhkov, the representative of a new, awakened Russia, repeatedly asked for "Truth" and "Justice." His reform plans contained nothing radical or revolutionary, but

---

[1] *Ibid.*, p. 48-49.

the very fact that he opposed the arbitrary activities of the
"tzar's servants" made him a person to be feared. Pososhkov
thoroughly understood that his measures would not be liked by the
nobles. His Poverty and Wealth was not written for publication;
it was rather a secret report made to the Tzar on the various
"evils" existing in his realm. In the petition accompanying his
book, Pososhkov requested: "Let my name remain unknown to envious
people, to informers and to lovers of evil! Because I have written
concerning them, they will discover that I am a 'tzar's orphan';
then I believe that they will not hesitate to wipe me off the face
of the earth." He was right! Poverty and Wealth was completed on
February 24, 1724, and on August 29, 1725, its author was arrested
and convicted as "guilty of a criminal act...". Pososhkov breathed
his last on February 1, 1726, while a prisoner in the Peter-Paul
Fortress.

Pososhkov's sympathies were above all with the merchant
class; nevertheless he condemned those European states where "power
is in the hands of the people, especially the merchants." The
monarch's rule should be as absolute as God's power. Although he
insisted that "the tzar must defend the peasants against the nobles,"
his aspirations were in reality modest. Pososhkov never expressed
the demand made by the ideologists of the French bourgeoisie: that
their class should become "everything." "The tzar must see to it

that the nation's wealth is so distributed that the nobles and the
military, as well as the peasants and the merchants, are all able
to pay their allotted share of the state's taxes."[1] To "guard the
peasants" meant to establish a definite system of taxation, but to
"guard the merchants" meant something more. Pososhkov reminded
Peter that in European countries the kings gave a special protection to their merchants; "whereas," he complained, "our courts
neglect completely the protection of the common people" (the "tzar's
orphans"). Such criticism of our judicial system makes up a large
part of his program. He asks for justice and, acting in accordance
with his philosophy of life, supports his demands with religious
arguments:

> God is Truth, and Truth He loves...How is truth to be achieved
> in the Russian courts of justice? For the sake of the happiness
> of all, our Great Tzar should establish one Court, one Justice
> for every one, for peasants and merchants, for rich and poor
> alike, for officer and soldier, without any discrimination
> whatsoever.

Pososhkov defended this idea of even-handed justice with
the fundamental principles of patriarchal monarchy: "A tzar is
the supreme judge; he is like God... In his court, as in the great
court of God, all are equal, the rich and the poor, the strong and
the weak. The judgment rendered is the same."[2] It is worth while

---

[1]
 Ibid., p. 189.
[2]
 Ibid., p. 257.

to note that Pososhkov came close to the modern idea of a universal
court of justice.[1] Pososhkov speculated further on the problem;
he realized that a new code of law was needed for such a court because the old laws had become obsolete and the old judges tended
to interpret those old laws as they saw fit... "It seems to me
that it would be a good idea to select some peasants to act as
lawmakers," he added.[2] He advised further that a new code of law
be presented for the approval of all, "so that none may acquire
any privileges, and equal justice may prevail for all."[3] After
writing down these thoughts, however, he began to fear that he
might be misunderstood by the tzar. He rationalized as follows:
there was no need to believe that, because he recommended the
plebiscite, he wanted in any way to diminish the tzar's authority.
The plebiscite was to be used only to fathom the true sentiment
of the people, but not to limit "His Highness' privileges." He
was absolutely sincere in his assertion.

Briknor made a great and incomprehensible mistake in ac-
cusing Pososhkov of proposing sweeping political changes at the
time he proposed the plebiscite and in comparing these demands with
those of Montesquieu and other French enlighteners. And yet,

1
  Pososhkov, Father's Testament, op. cit., pp. 184-185.
2
  Pososhkov, Works, op. cit., vol. 1, p. 76.
3
  Ibid.

Pososhkov was the same "Moscow progressive" working for reconstruction; he still did not look into the future but was always turning to the past, because such was the logic of social relations of Moscow's patriarchal monarchy.

The bureaucratic administrators were loading "impossible burdens" on the shoulders of the taxpayers of Russia. Every one not blinded by the self-interest or prejudices of this class could observe these conditions.[1] The sad part of it was that the discovery of the evil did not lead to immediate remedial measures. Suppose that this proposed plebiscite of all the people had granted a new code of law to Russia! The administrators of such law would still have been chosen from the class of the "tzar's servants." Who was to stop them from continuing their accustomed evil practices?

It has been impossible to find in all of old Moscow's annals an answer to such a question; Pososhkov's own reply is quite unsatisfactory. First, he advised prayer. Then, he recommended stern steps: "In plain words, it is impossible to establish honest

---

[1] That this social and political order of Russia was responsible for retarding the development of her economic forces was observed not only by Pososhkov. Kilbourger wrote: "The Russians are in a position to prosper ten times as much as foreigners, not only because of the favorable geographic position of their country, but also because they have special talent for commerce." See his "Kurzer Unterricht" and other articles in Buchings Magazin für die neue Historie und Geographie. Hamburg, 1769, pt. 3, p. 249.

justice until one or two hundred judges are removed; the evil of
corrupt courts is too strongly rooted in the Russian soil."[1] It
was the same bureaucracy from which the judges were appointed for
a consideration that had to punish these old reprobate law officers.
Would it severely punish its own appointees? Pososhkov doubted it,
and, in order to improve the situation somewhat, he recommended
choosing judges from among the lowly born, not the nobles. The
nobles had too many connections that would interfere with their
just administration of the law.

These "poison ivy seeds" (as the judges and other members
of the department of justice were nicknamed) were never outstanding figures because of their noble birth, but they knew how to
twist the laws to suit their ends. The basic reason for the frequent miscarriage of justice in the Muscovite state was the fact
that the common people had no legal standing in the courts. Pososhkov never touched upon this fundamental question in his discussions
on justice. His source of inspiration, the Moscow tradition, had
never known anything that could by a stretch be called a human right.
He could only advise prayer and recommend the use of stern and cruel
methods toward corrupt judges.

The "authorities" could readily persecute the mass of the
population because the vast majority were illiterate. Accordingly,
Pososhkov counselled that the children of the peasants be taught to

---

[1]
 Pososhkov, Works, op. cit., vol. 1, pp. 85-86.

read and write - unquestionably a step forward. It is, without doubt, an exaggeration to ascribe to Pososhkov advocacy of compulsory universal education. He remarked: "It would be good to have in every village at least one literate person."[1] This could by no means be called compulsory education. One must admit, to be sure, that Pososhkov has not always expressed himself clearly; and when Pogodin chose to alter his orthography, he deprived research students of the opportunity to study Pososhkov's manuscripts.

From this educational proposal let us turn to another, having no direct relation to it, but one which interested Pososhkov greatly and which formed the basis of one of his characteristic law projects. His recommendation, motivated by the aim to develop Russia's productive forces, was: "To round up all paupers and vagabonds on the streets and to train them in weaving and spinning, so that they may be useful to the State in its factories." Pososhkov also advised that rights to conscript labor be granted to private employers.[2] This recommendation reminds us of the conscription laws of Europe: the English edicts of 1530 and 1547, the French administrative ordinance of 1777, the articles of Charles V for the Netherlands in 1537, and the first edict of the Dutch states and cities, posted in the United Provinces on June 25, 1649, etc.[3]

---

[1] Ibid., pp. 175-176.
[2] Ibid., p. 151.
[3] Karl Marx, Capital, translated by Samuel Moore and Edward Aveling, Chicago, 1919, vol. 1, pp. 806, 808.

In the present case, there is agreement between the ideas
of our Moscow progressive and those of European administrators. Of
course, we are not allowed to assume that he was ahead of Western
lawmakers, because his measures, proposed in the 17th century, had
already been in operation in Europe for two centuries. It is somewhat strange for Pososhkov to have forsaken the old Moscow attitude
that paupers are "an ornament of the Church, brethren of Christ,
pilgrims of the world etc.,"[1] and to have proposed this scheme for
the development of the State's productive forces.[2]

Extremely practical man that he was, Pososhkov did not
speculate idly and studied only the immediate economic problems of
Russia. The means for solving those problems satisfactorily were
in the hands of the Russian tzars and the administrators of the
State. Pososhkov thought that the State must, for its own sake,
methodically supervise the State's economic life with a view to
educating the population. On this point, his views coincided with
those of the mercantilists of Western Europe. But his proposals
for supervision were tinged with the usual Muscovite color. The
enforcement of these measures should be placed in the hands of a
special police force which was to be given authority to fine and

---

[1] I. Prijov, The Paupers in Holy Russia, Moscow, 1869, p. 58.
[2] Pososhkov, Father's Testament, op. cit., p. 169.

thrash all stubborn nonconformists.[1] According to Pososhkov, the
whip is the only effective means by which the administration can
educate the Russian people; this view conformed completely with
that of Peter the Great and his "nestlings." Thus, even those who
tried to reform and change Moscow's traditional order were inevitably influenced by that very tradition.

Pososhkov worked out and presented a complete program of
applied political economy. It contained all the important features
of the mercantilism adopted by the Russia of his day. It is especially remarkable that a merchant should have been responsible
for such a plan. Naturally, all Russians of that time who were
interested in economic policy, including Peter the Great, were
avowed mercantilists. We doubt, however, that any of Peter's "Learned
Guard" had thought out the ramifications of this program as clearly
and systematically as Pososhkov. Brikner observed that, with the
exception of Pososhkov, not one of Peter's "nestlings" could be
called a student of economics.[2] His assertion is correct; but when
he credited Pososhkov with certain modern and progressive ideas of
which he could not even have dreamed in the Russia of his time,
Brikner is sadly mistaken. Actually, Pososhkov made no discoveries

_____

1
Klyuchevsky, Russian History, pt. 3, pp. 449-450.
2
Brikner, Ivan Pososhkov, pt. 1, "Pososhkov as an Economist,"
St. Petersburg, 1876, p. 67.

whatsoever, either in the field of economic theory or in that of
practical economics; he only brought to light such mercantilist
views as had been formulated much earlier in Western Europe. Of
course, he communicated these theories in terms of the social and
political traditions of Russia's patriarchal monarchy. When Brikner
made the statement that no one but Pososhkov - neither Vinius,
Kourbatov, Genning nor Kirillov, not even Tatishchev - could have
written such a work as Poverty and Wealth, he is right once more,
but only in a limited sense. A man of Tatishchev's scholarship
would probably have speculated more profoundly on economic matters,
had he considered the subject at all. His reasoning power was undoubtedly greater than Pososhkov's, to say nothing of his education.
On the other hand, in speaking of "Truth," that is, the administration of justice, to which the greater part of Poverty and Wealth is
dedicated, Tatishchev's conception of the nobleman would have made
it impossible for him to see many aspects of life to which our Moscow
"merchant" was sensitive. This very status was Pososhkov's most
powerful asset in observing realistically "the impossible burdens"
of the people; such was the nature of his observations that our
Moscow "progressive" had to be jailed for uttering them; up to the
time of the reforms of Alexander II, such views were considered
dangerous by Russia's bureaucrats.

Pososhkov was never known to shake the foundations of society; he wanted only to propagate the old traditions of Moscow, enlarge them and place them at the disposal of the working masses. The fact that Pososhkov was a "tzar's orphan" and not a "tzar's servant" influenced negatively not only his intellectual development but also the fate of his humanitarian proposals. His social status made it impossible for him to understand Europeans and their civilization; he could not even grasp the limited knowledge of the West gained by Peter's "nestlings." He was a self-made man of the old Moscow school. When this self-taught merchant devised some schemes which he believed valuable to the whole State, he had to overcome almost insurmountable obstacles in order to bring them to the attention of the proper authorities.

Peter's reforms were carried out by the nobles. In the case of Pososhkov, we are dealing with a man who was in sympathy with these reforms but had no opportunity to put them into effect. There is much pessimism in Pososhkov's report about the execution of these reforms: "We all know, we can all see how hard our great Monarch is working; he pulls his heavy load up-hill, with only a few to assist him, while millions are pulling in the opposite direction. How then can his work run smoothly?"[1] This oft-quoted phrase

---

[1] Pososhkov, Works, op. cit., vol. 1, p. 95.

describes perfectly Peter's attempt to bring law and order to his
land. Pososhkov's words, however, indicate that all was not well
in "renovated" Russia. It is this remark that distinguishes
Pososhkov from the long list of professional panegyrists of Peter's
reform.

2. MICHAIL VASILIEVICH LOMONOSOV[1]

Russia's educational system in the 18th century was
determined by the autocratic nature of her government. The "service
class," especially those "near the throne," had every opportunity
to satisfy their thirst for knowledge. In fact, education was made
compulsory for all members of the noble class and for court favorites. Not only were all doors of the university open to them but
they had the educational positions at their "command." Thus Kiril
Rasoomovsky, at the age of eighteen, was appointed president of
the Academy of Science. By making education of the nobility obligatory, Peter's reform, however, changed nothing in the status of
ordinary taxpaying Russians; the doors of the schools were closed
to commoners. As an exception, the administration admitted a few
children of commoners to the schools, because there were not enough
educated noblemen to fill the needs of the State; but even then,

---

[1]
Lomonosov, Michail Vasilievich, 1712-1765, the "peasant from
Archangel"; Russia's first scholar; historian, naturalist, chemist,
educator, author and poet; nicknamed: "The Russian University." -
Translator's note.

those sons of commoners appointed to State positions were not allowed to mingle with the children of the nobility. When the University of Moscow was founded, two preparatory schools were opened; one for the nobility, another for commoners. In St. Petersburg, where only one preparatory school for the Academy of Science existed, the law of 1750 seated the "children of the nobility and of other privileged classes apart from the children of commoners."[1] From all indications the aristocracy valued these privileges highly. We know that even the learned Tatishchev insisted that the gentry should be "separated from the lowly," in educational matters. Finally, it must be remembered that the children of the great mass of serfs were not among those commoners fortunate enough to be admitted to the schools.

It seems that Nekrassov was too optimistic when he wrote in his "Schoolboy":

> The land must be still prolific
> And a country must be still alive
> When there are born one after another
> So many great men....

Undoubtedly Russian land "was and is prolific." But one must admit, with regret, that talented commoners had almost no chance to develop their mental powers and become the "great"...The socio-political system barred the Russian masses from the "Temple

---

[1]
V. Kalash, Sketches on the History of Schools and Education, Moscow, 1902, p. 96.

of Science." This is the bitter truth. There is a "legend" that
Michail Lomonosov, "the peasant from Archangel" (the hero of the
quoted poem) resorted to false representation in order to gain admittance to the schools. It is said that he was accepted in the
Slavonic-Greek-Latin Academy as "a son of a priest"; another version
calls him "a nobleman's son." (Only members of these two classes
were admitted to this school.) Later, fearing punishment for mis-
representation, he confessed, according to the "legend," to Feofan
Prokopovich and was told: "Do not be afraid; if you are denounced
as an impostor, I shall defend you." We doubt the facts in this
story. But "se non è vero, è ben trovato." There is a fragment of
truth in it. We know, too, that of the "Learned Guards," Prokopovich,
more than any other member, realized the great need of education in
Russia. Our story forgets, however, that the same "Guards" were
steeped in the prejudices of the old gentry. The legend does describe accurately the hopeless position of the many talented young
men who were tempted by the light of science, but who could not
enjoy the good fortune of being given the educational advantages of
the privileged.

The question thus arises: how could young Michail Lomonosov,
in spite of his peasant origin, have become the best known Russian
scholar of the 18th century? Of course, "nature" helped by endow-
ing him with great talent; but this talent had to be brought to
light and be put to use in life. In order to find an explanation,
we must, above all, remember the praiseworthy persistence of which

Lomonosov was so proud in later years. (He certainly was "per-

sistent.") In a letter to Ivan Shuvalov, he says:

> When I was at the Spasskoy Academy (another name for the
> Academy of Moscow), there was strong pressure on all sides
> to take me away from school; at times this pressure was al-
> most unbearable. My father, who had no other children, com-
> plained constantly that I left him alone. And then the great
> poverty! I was allowed only three kopeks a day; I could not
> spend more than a kopek for bread and a kopek for kvass, and
> the last kopek went for paper, shoes and other necessaries...
> I lived this way for five years while pursuing my studies.
> They wrote me from my village back home that a bride was wait-
> ing for me; on the other hand, the schoolboys were yelling:
> "Look, what a dumbbell! Twenty years old, and only now he
> wants to take up Latin!"

From the foregoing we perceive a great deal of commend-

able persistence in our "peasant from Archangel," but still it does

not solve the problem of how a peasant boy, no matter how talented

he might be, could enter school. The following explanation is

offered. Lomonosov was born in the North of Russia; that part of

the country, far away from the central Moscow provinces, was not

under the influence of Moscow's customs. Although the Church was

in possession of large tracts of land and owned serfs, there were

no fiefs (pomestie). This absence of fiefs had a beneficial in-

fluence on the character and customs of the local population. The

Northerners, since the time of the "Great Novgorod," were very

mobile and independent. Independence goes hand in hand with culture.

We know that the peasant Schubny taught Lomonosov how to read and

write and induced him to continue his studies in the Moscow Academy.

From Christopher Dudin, another of his fellow villagers, he borrowed

the Book of Psalms (put into verse by Simeon Polotzky), Smotritzky's
Grammar and Magnitzky's Arithmetic. The fondest hope of a peasant
from the province of Moscow, Pososhkov, was that there should be
at least one literate man for each village. In the town of Denisovka,
Lomonosov's birthplace, this dream became a reality. The fact that
there were educated men in his home village helped our genius on
his road to the university.

Prior to learning how to read, young Lomonosov had learned
how to travel; he knew how to overcome the hardships of travel on
land and on sea. His father was a fisherman, and he often took his
son along on his trips. Some of our historians think that it was
the glorious phenomenon of nature in the North that inspired the
talented youngster and planted in his soul the belief in the existence of the Almighty Creator, which he so often voiced. Probably
there is some truth in it, although his belief in God, as we shall
see later, could be explained differently. These hard and adventur-
ous travels made a man of the youth and gave him his "noble perseverance." Had Lomonosov been born in some village of Central
Russia, he would not have been able to travel with his father beyond the limits of the landlord's estate; in all probability, he
then would never have been inspired to go to Moscow. The very idea
would have seemed a nightmare, and even if he had tried to go, the
laws prohibiting admittance of serfs to the schools would have
placed the most serious obstacles in his way. It seems that the

"peasant from Archangel" became a famous scholar not only by "his and God's whim," but because he was a peasant from Archangel, a peasant of the coast line, who never bore the chains of serfdom.

Now let us look at the whole matter from a different point of view. On the Northern coast we did not have the tzar's "men of service," so that there could be no cause for class struggle; consequently, the country had neither the ambiance of oppression nor the temper of revolution. In the time of the "Turmoil" (1600-1613), when Bolotnikov called a general uprising of serfs and of free peasants, the people of the seacoast did not respond, but, on the contrary, gave their support to the Moscow government of Tzar Vasily. Their spirit of independence had nothing revolutionary in character, nothing that aimed at the destruction of the basis of government.

And there is nothing revolutionary about Lomonosov. His boyhood in the village by the sea left unforgettable imprints on his soul. These impressions were born of the severe Northern climate and of man's struggle for existence against nature. Social relations never inspired in Lomonosov an interest similar to that displayed by Pososhkov. Lomonosov's perseverance made him independent, a man who could hold up his head proudly even in those dark times when educated commoners, like the unfortunate Tred'yakovsky humbly bent their heads to a "patron." Assuredly, Lomonosov had to solicit the patronage of Ivan Shuvalov; no one could live without a protector at that time. Still, even while trying to find a patron,

Lomonosov knew how to preserve his independence. "I do not want

to become the fool of anyone," he wrote to Shuvalov, "not even of

the Lord, who gave me my brains, unless He takes them back."[1] His

spirit of personal independence fitted in very well with an almost

complete indifference to the contemporary social structure. Bulich

remarked that Lomonosov did not see the dark side of Peter's reform.

He could have said more: Lomonosov did not even see the dark side

of Russia's contemporary social order. In this respect our highly

talented and cultured scholar from the seacoast always lagged be-

hind the "Moscow merchant," the self-made Pososhkov, who passion-

ately sought the eternal truth in social relations.

It seems that the exclusion of the children of serfs from

the schools should have inspired in Lomonosov a severe condemnation

of the law. Indeed, his own experience taught him how hard it was

for the children of taxpayers to enter the schools. He also knew

that in other countries of Europe there was no social discrimina-

tion in educational institutions. He wrote about the academic laws

of 1747:

> Other European states have many educated people of different
> social levels. Prospective students are not discriminated
> against, nor are they forbidden to enter institutions of
> learning. In the universities the students are respected for

---

[1]
From manuscripts collected by Bilyarsky, the Academician, for
Lomonosov's biography.

what they accomplish, and no one is interested in asking who
their parents are. Here in Russia, where there are only a
few scholars, the nobility has a monopoly on education, and
the taxpayers' children are forbidden to study. Possibly the
lawmakers thought that the burden on the state would be too
great if it lost the head tax of forty altin [$1.20] a year
for each student!

Although Lomonosov criticized the lawmakers, he did not

say, as Pososhkov surely would have done, that taxpayers have a

right to study. He only wanted to obtain some privileges for the

wealthier part of the population. He asked: "Is it the fault of

some taxpayers that they have capital and can educate their children?

Why is it that education is forbidden to good taxpayers and serfs

alike?"

What does this statement mean? Does it, perhaps, imply

that Lomonosov, despairing of obtaining everything, would have been

satisfied with achieving at least something? Or does it mean that

Lomonosov had the "good taxpayers" closer to his heart than the serfs?

Suchopluyev recently wrote that in Lomonosov's Memorandum

on how to Bring About an Increase in the Birth Rate, he "requested

the limitation of the rights of the nobility."[1] The character of

this request can be learned from Lomonosov's recommendation on the

subject of runaway serfs who escaped from the border provinces of

Russia and were thus lost to the State, becoming, in Lomonosov's

_____

[1]
"Lomonosov's Outlook on Population Policies," Lomonosov's Collection,
1911, p. 193.

phrase, "living corpses." The government tried to prevent the exodus by increasing the border patrols. Lomonosov thought that this method was inadequate, because - again we use his own expression - "it is hard to plug up such a great hole." According to him, there is only one effective method: kindness. "This desertion is the result of the oppression of the peasants by the landowners and of frequent mobilizations; it seems to me that it would be better to ease the tax burden and stop mobilizing in the border provinces."[1]

This is the only place in his memoranda where our writer makes reference to the status of serfs. But he disregards essentials for the sake of detail. It is amazing that Lomonosov did not present a single project dealing with the limitation of the rights of the landowners, not even for the border provinces. He only suggested that the tax burden be eased and the hardship of mobilization be alleviated, and that then only the absolutely necessary measures should be taken. Undoubtedly, he promised some constructive measures in his Memorandum on Correcting the People's Morals. This memorandum is lost, however, and we have no reason to expect that Lomonosov expressed there a broader outlook on the problems of the State in dealing with serfs.

1
Discussions in the Moscow University Society of Lovers of Russian Literature, Moscow, 1871, pp. 85-86.

In the beginning of the 1840's, the editors of Muscovite published the Memorandum on the Increase in the Birth Rate with this remark: "There is no problem of government or population to which the great scholar and writer did not turn his attention. He had an opinion on everything and had solutions for all these problems."[1] This is true. There was no limit to the subjects that absorbed his attention. In his letter to Shuvalov he said that he had worked out many other memoranda "for the common weal," which could be formulated as follows: (1) How to bring about an increase in the birth rate; (2) how to overcome idleness; (3) how to improve morals by education; (4) how to improve agriculture; (5) how to improve handicrafts and applied arts and how to disseminate such knowledge; (6) how merchants can increase their profits; (7) how to improve the State's economy; (8) how the military sciences can be cultivated in times of long peace.

Pushkin states very properly that Lomonosov was "the first Russian University." We must add, however, that not all the faculties of this remarkable one-man university functioned with equal success. The natural sciences were his specialty. In this field he was a deep and original thinker. In the field of sociology, on the other hand, his views on what constituted the common weal were shallow and borrowed. A careful reader of his Memorandum on How

[1]

Muscovite, 1842, bk. 1, "Material for the History of Russian Literature," p. 126, footnote. Lomonosov's Memorandum was published here with omissions.

to Bring About an Increase in the Birth Rate would say that in a
work of this sort the critical remarks on the foundation of our
social order should have been omitted. We know already how super-
ficially he solved the problem of the status of serfs in our border
provinces. Another truly astonishing remark in this connection
may be quoted. When he proposed the solution of the serfs' problems,
he added the following sentence: "Because of religious difficulties
many Russian old-believers emigrated into Votkaland (Poland). Is
it possible to bring them back with the aid of our military expedi-
tion there?"[1] It appears as if Lomonosov advised the government
to use the army to return runaway serfs from Poland. No doubt,
such proposed measures were not humanitarian. We have a right to
expect something more noble from Lomonosov, but his understanding
of these problems was unquestionably poor.[2]

In trying to explain Lomonosov's reasons, Suchopluyev
states that our author was a follower of the eudaemonist philosophy,
a philosophy systematized by Christian Wolf. Suchopluyev explains
Wolf's credo: "It is the duty and the right of the supreme state
power to assist in attaining general happiness and to further the
common weal through administrative measures in the name of natural
law. Like Wolf, Lomonosov believed in the absolute truth of natural

---

[1]
Lomonosov, Discussion, pub. 3, p. 85, Memorandum marked November 1,
1761, that is, at the time of the Seven Years' War.

[2]
Moscow Collection, p. 209.

law and overestimated the omnipotence of the government."[1] If we
accept this hypothesis, then indeed this systematic eudaemonism
had to uphold the "police" state! What a great and humorous de-
lusion![2] This was Wolf's doctrine, however, and Lomonosov followed
him in this instance, as he did in many others. Otherwise, our
great scholar would not have given such advice on the subject under
discussion. If his social horizon had extended farther than the
limits of the police system, he would not have seen the status of
the serf only through governmental eyes. Like Wolf, Lomonosov's
ideal was the police-administered state having at its head an enlightened absolute monarch. The measures recommended by Lomonosov
in this memorandum reveal unshakable trust in the omnipotence of a
well-disposed and enlightened administration. Lomonosov's faith
was further strengthened by the inspiring greatness of Peter.

Lomonosov realized the many obstacles in the way of correcting Russia's shortcomings, but he did not consider these obstacles
insurmountable. "Has not much been accomplished? People shave,
wear German clothes and display courtesy toward foreigners; they
have done away with the boyars, the patriarchs and the Strelitzes;

---

[1]
Lomonosov's scheme was already tried by one administration. In
1733-1734, the Russian military authorities took Russian runaway
peasants from Poland by force... The idea of easing the life of
Russian peasants in the borderline countries was expressed before
Lomonosov. In 1735, A. Buturlin, the governor of Smolensk, sent
a report to the Administration on this subject. Compare Soloviev,
History of Russia, Book 4, p. 1435.
[2]
We must add that Wolf was not such a blind adherent of eudaemonism
as Suchopluyov believes.

they have even established a senate, a Holy Synod and a regular

army, and have founded a new national capital on barren land. The

celebration of New Year's day has been changed to a different month.

Surely, the Russian people are flexible!"[1]

The manner in which Lomonosov linked the Russians' adapt-

ability to Russian custom is curious. He believed that our fasting

periods were too long and therefore harmful to the nation's health:

> Our poor stomachs, after being subjected for lengthy periods
> to unwholesome food, are suddenly called upon to absorb into
> a weakened system a great deal of rich food; the stomach,
> lacking an adequate amount of juices, cannot digest these foods
> and consequently becomes poisoned. Many deaths are caused by
> constipation and blood poisoning....

As proof of his contention, he points to the vital sta-

tistics of the Church, which show that more koutya (the traditional

food for the dead, made of wheat and honey) was used by the priests

immediately after the fasting periods than at any other time during

the year.

The custom of fasting originated in Southern countries,

he stated, where the climate made it necessary. The Russian climate

differs greatly from that of the Mediterranean. Besides, we must

remember that:

> God is more pleased when we have a clear conscience than when
> we have our bellies stuffed with spoiled fish... And would
> not a man who ate ashes, shavings or clay and stood on his

---

[1]
Lomonosov, Memorandum, p. 81.

head during the whole of the Lent period, be condemned as bad
if he did not worship the Lord in the accepted fashion?

All sensible people must approve of the foregoing statement. Lomonosov continues his Memorandum in the same vein; for
example, he condemns the custom of baptizing children in cold water.
He recommends that "they be baptized in water having about the temper-
ature of summer weather."[1] He also complains that Russia has no
trained midwives and that the people know nothing about children's
diseases. He sees in forced and unequal marriages the greatest
obstacle to an increase in population. By "inequality" he means a
great difference in age between bridegroom and bride. He thinks
that the bride should never be more than two years older than the
groom, and the groom's age should not exceed the bride's by more
than fifteen years. A 'forced" marriage is a marriage against the
will of either of the parties or of both... "Where there is no
love, there is little hope for having children."[2] He was against
young people taking the veil; men under fifty and women under forty-
five years of age should not be allowed to take vows. He wanted
the government to establish "orphan homes" for illegitimate children.
All of these wise projects have as their base one central idea:
the welfare of the State. The private interests of people are not
involved in Lomonosov's schemes. Moreover, his concern for the State

---

[1] Ibid., p. 81.
[2] Ibid., p. 84.

made him advocate only such measures as would interfere least with the established social traditions of Russia. Lomonosov might have aroused the ire of the clergy by his liberal views on Lent and also by his caustic remarks about their beards, but in matters of politics he was always a full-fledged and sincere conservative.

Wolf was a conservative in the same political sense, although he was much disliked by the orthodox Protestants and the Pietists in his own country. It would be a mistake, however, to ascribe Lomonosov's conservatism to the influence of Wolf. He was much too independent to subject himself without criticism to anyone's influence. He accepted Wolf's conception of natural order in the world, since he himself had no inclination to criticize the existing social order. What distinguishes German philosophy from the French is the spirit of compromise that dominated the thinkers of Germany. Wolf's conceptions were an attempt to eliminate from enlightened philosophy all weighty and controversial questions - the very questions that might bring him into conflict with conditions as they existed in Germany. In order to avoid such clashes, liberal thinkers had to declare peace between religion and science. This compromise had been proclaimed by Leibniz, who spent much time and energy in hopeless attempts to build a theoretical foundation for this alliance. Wolf tried to establish this peace even more energetically than Leibniz. He firmly insisted that the stories of the Old and New Testaments were not in opposition to reason and common

sense. Wolf devoted much space to the physico-theological proof
of the existence of God. In this respect Lomonosov followed closely
in Wolf's footsteps. Here are a few lines from his "Morning Reflection on God's Greatness":

> Send, Oh Creator! Science's keen light
> To one who lives in darkness complete;
> Teach me Thy infinite wisdom,
> So I may act according to Thy Will;
> And having observed Thy works, Oh Lord!
> I shall glorify You, my heavenly Father!

Even Voltaire eagerly availed himself of physico-theological evidence to prove the existence of God. He was a confirmed
deist, although during his whole life he waged relentless war to
"crush the infamous tyranny" of ecclesiasticism.

Lomonosov never had such ideas. His realistic discussions
on the benefits derived from fasting during Lent might have proved
distasteful to the clergy, but they were never dangerous to the
Church. If Lomonosov was not exactly ultraconservative in his relations to the Church, he was at least as conservative as Tzar Peter,
his ideal monarch-enlightener. With little ceremony Peter assumed
complete control over the Russian clergy. Although he subordinated
the clerical hierarchy to the authority of the State, he would not
tolerate any criticism of Church dogma.

Lomonosov never attacked or doubted this dogma. In this
matter, too, he was not inclined to "shake any foundations." He
was sure that scientific truth and religious faith "are two sisters,

daughters of the same Heavenly Father"; they could "never quarrel...."
Did he have to spend his childhood among the great natural scenes
of the North in order to develop such a conviction in his mature
years? No! All the German philosophers of the school of enlightenment were defenders of the same principles, although they had never
visited that Northern country. They arrived at this conclusion because they had none of the French spirit of opposition that so often
brought about quarrels between the Church and science in France....

Lomonosov did not have this French spirit either. His
poetical "Reflections on God's Greatness" are certainly sincere.
They are inspired by the Muses. In works of this kind Lomonosov
is more the poet than in his odes; this is especially true when,
in the capacity of a naturalist, he observes the universe.

His language is heavy, as was the case in many verses,
even the best, of that time. Still, there runs a comic vein through
his poem, "Evening Reflection on God's Greatness!"

> Soft veils cover the ending day
> Darkenihg doubts sweep o'er the fields
> And shadows creep across the hills.
> The sun's dying rays begin to vanish...
> And now bright stars fill the sky;
> Oh, bottomless pit! oh, countless stars!
> ....
> And to man's ears, Reason whispers:
> "There are many such flaming suns,
> Nations appear like sands of the sea -
> Time is endless with myriads of years...."

It is strange that Pushkin, with his exceptional critical
sense, who, in general, gave such correct estimates of the activities

of Lomonosov, missed this phase of his genius. If, as Pushkin remarked, inspiration is the ability of the soul to receive impressions,
then Lomonosov's scientific conception of the cosmos made him sus-
ceptible to the influence of the picturesque and severe Northern
country.

An advocate of enlightenment, Lomonosov could not but bow
to the tzar who "saw the necessity of promoting all the sciences in
the Fatherland...."[1] But his exaggerated praises of the first
Russian emperor leave the modern reader with a certain disgust. "If
there were need of finding a man - a godlike man -, I could only
point to Peter the Great." It seems impossible to give greater
praise than this. Yet, Lomonosov is able to go still further when
he says in the same article:

> For his great service to the people of Russia he is named the
> "Father of his Country." This title is too small for Peter.
> How else can one honor the Father of the most gracious Tzarina,
> who, having taken over the throne, has defeated the enemies
> of her empire and brought peace to Europe?[2]

To think that the title of "Father of his Country" is insufficient for Peter because he was the father of Elizabeth! Such
a statement even surpasses Lomonosov's customary magniloquence,
especially since he holds that "style in eulogistic orations must
be solemn and magnificent, though gracious and delightful."[3] We

---

1
Lomonosov, Works, published by the Academy of Science, vol. 4, p. 68.
2
Ibid., p. 390.
3
Lomonosov, Works, op. cit., vol. 3, p. 70.

must admit that Lomonosov's eulogistic "style" is far from delightful; it is really obnoxious. It reminds us of the panegyrics of
Pliny the Younger and other Roman authors. A sense of shame comes
over us in having to compare our "Archangel peasant" with the orators
of Rome.

There is no doubt that the reign of Elizabeth gave to some
people a chance to "breathe," after the throttling misrule of Biron.
We now know that there was little improvement in the general conditions of the country. Many contemporaries of Lomonosov saw this
very well.[1] Could it be that he, observant as he was, did not see
it? And if he did, what was the source of his ecstasy? How could
he have sung of the "blessings of his days"? It must be added that
he was not the only person who was fond of writing panegyrics, but
this would be an insufficient explanation. Lomonosov was so much
greater than his contemporaries that he could afford to ignore the
established order. He could, indeed, talk to Ivan Shuvalov, his
patron of noble rank, in a manner never before used by a commoner.
But to write about Peter and his imperial daughter was something
quite different. A spirit of personal independence may have governed
Lomonosov's relations with Shuvalov, but such temper was insufficient
to grasp and understand the dark chapters of Peter's reform, and

---

[1]
The envoy of Holland wrote in 1757: "Society in Russia represents
a terrible picture of dissolution and disorder. The Empress sees
and hears only Shuvalov (probably P. P. Shuvalov). She has
nothing to worry about and continues to live as irresponsibly as
ever. She has virtually led her empire to destruction." The
Russian Court a Hundred Years Ago, St. Petersburg, p. 73.

the black pages of Elizabeth's reign; to understand these, one had
to be capable of thinking in terms of social phenomena, a quality
completely lacking in Lomonosov. Although great as a naturalist,
he was most naïve in political matters.[1]

Lomonosov argues that Russia, because of her vastness and
her era of peace under Elizabeth's wise rule, would be a happy dwell-
ing place for the Muses. This argument is certainly weak from the
viewpoint of cultural history.[2] This is the first time, however,
that we find the idea expressed that Russia possesses geographical
advantages denied to Western Europe, benefits which will in time enable her to outstrip the rest of Europe. This thought became quite
current later. Aspirations of this sort were cherished above all
by our great innovators in their dreams of social and political reforms.

When we read Pososhkov's book on Poverty and Wealth, we
realize how deeply Pososhkov was affected by the misfortunes of the
taxpaying population of Russia. We find no such feeling in the works
of Lomonosov. There is no doubt that he loved Russia and her people,

---

[1]
Prior to his praise of Empress Elizabeth, Lomonosov had also sung
encomiums to her predecessor, Anna, in his Ode on the Capture of
Chotin. Much naïveté was needed to forget the revolution of
November, 1741 (which raised Elizabeth to the throne).

[2]
Lomonosov's geographical argument reminds us of Gogol's explanation
(in the first part of Dead Souls): "Only in our boundless land
could limitless thought be born! Only Russia could bear and rear
a viking - she has endless spaces in which men can work and grow."

but Lomonosov's childhood impressions were different from those of
Pososhkov, and he tried to serve Russia not by curing her social
ills but by propagating enlightenment. All of his grandiose praises
of Peter's daughter were but a means of winning over the Empress
to the cause of education. In his Word of Praise of November 26,
1747, on the anniversary of her reign, Lomonosov outlined a broad
educational program while singing a paean to the glory of the Tzarina:

> Not only are we fortunate enough to have Her Majesty's coopera-
> tion in studying the secrets of nature and the miraculous deeds
> of the Wise Creator, her patronage of teaching institutions and
> her graciousness in observing the fruits of our efforts, and
> not only do students receive everything that is necessary for
> their education, but her work encompasses a broad plan for the
> general welfare. Throughout all of Peter's Russia, science is
> at work and no man is denied the benefits of schooling.

The purpose of this speech was to improve the welfare of
the country through the development of schools; it is similar to
the programs of leaders in other nations. But each country's educational system is molded by the social and political forms existing
there. During the first half of the 18th century, our enlighteners
did not include any plans for social reform in their school programs.
Lomonosov is a typical representative of this group. He persisted
in advocating education for his countrymen, but never did he dare
to suggest improvements in government. When compared with this
Petersburg enlightener, Pososhkov, the "Moscow progressive," was
indeed a man to be feared, since he insisted on effecting radical
changes in government.

Still, the administration was not always pleased with
Lomonosov's utterances or activities. Only recently had Russia begun to adopt Western European enlightenment. Scientists were asked
to come to Russia, but not all of the invited were true scholars.
They actually abused the privilege of their stay in Russia and tried
to monopolize education. Lomonosov and Pososhkov noticed the exploitation of their countrymen and attempted to free Russia from
foreign control. Their efforts, however, did not arouse a dislike
for the foreigners. It could not have been otherwise, as the very
character of Lomonosov explains the failure of his efforts. He
could observe the burdens of the serfs and slaves passively, but
he never missed a chance to show that the foreigners were mercenary
in their educational work. He could not control his temper when
dealing with this question; he aroused such resentment that efforts
were made to chastise him and even to threaten his life. If he escaped punishment or assassination, it was only out of respect for
his deep learning.

Lomonosov addressed the Russian youth in the name of the
Empress Elizabeth: "I want to see the Russian Academy filled with
sons of Russia who aim at scientific achievement, so that Russia
may become glorious. This was the desire of My parents and this is
My will." He outlines at length the list of problems awaiting
solution: "No one has yet written about the deeds of My forefathers;
none has yet sung, as it should be sung, the glory of Peter. Enrich

your outlook; enrich Russian literature." These are the themes
for future historians and writers and here is something for future
scientists: "In My great Empire there is unestimated wealth and
natural resources which are lying idle, awaiting only the hands of
craftsmen. Study diligently the natural sciences, and you will earn
My grace."

The thought that Russia must learn to stand on her own
feet in the field of abstract and applied sciences seldom left
Lomonosov: "The Motherland, ever since it carried you in her womb,
expects you to become like those invited from abroad.,. You have
the privilege of being active Russians. Show by your work, inspired
by Her Majesty, that Russia can have her own Platos and her own
Newtons." Practical knowledge acquired under such conditions would
help in the development of the country's productive forces. This
notion was dear to his heart and was expressed many times.

Even on his deathbed, Lomonosov was preoccupied with the
thought of sending Russian students abroad. It must be admitted
that he showed more enthusiasm for the sciences and education than
all the other members of the "Learned Guard." Kantemir considered
service to the state much more important than literary pursuits.
To Lomonosov service to his country meant working indefatigably for
the development of Russian science and enlightenment. Our great
peasant deserves special honor for his devotion to such a noble task.

Lomonosov considered it his duty to "uncover the ancient history of the Russian nation and the glorious deeds of our rulers." That is why his Ancient History of Russia follows the trend of his Word of Praise. While he was devoting himself to his historical studies, Lomonosov could not forgive the disdainful attitude of foreigners towards Russians and their land. He wanted to glorify Russian history so that "everyone would find in the Slavic sagas deeds as magnificent as those of ancient Greece and Rome; then Russia need never again be humiliated." Pososhkov would probably have understood and approved Lomonosov's sentiments. In comparing the history of Russia with that of Rome, Lomonosov found some similarities (as few as these are!). The period of Roman kings corresponds to the period of the first great princes of Russia. The early Roman republic resembles the period of "division of our land into different principalities, domains of princes and free cities...." The period of emperors seemed to Lomonosov to correspond to the absolutism of the Moscow period. There is only this difference: Rome rose while a republic, whereas in the time of the emperors it began to decline. Russia, on the other hand, almost came to destruction because of too much freedom; it was saved only by absolutism, which brought strength and glory to Russia. Manifestly, there is too much naïveté and too little science in this parallel. Soloviev rightfully calls the comparison "strange." According to Lomonosov, Peter raised Russia to the heights of glory. Consequently, it was only natural to put full confidence in the enlightened activities

of Russia's tzars. Many Russian progressives held this opinion

long after Lomonosov's death.

I repeat that Lomonosov's principal vocation was natural

science. During the 19th century many important discoveries were

credited to him by Russia's naturalists. It is recorded, for

instance, that Lomonosov was the first to explain the formation of

coal and the origin of amber. Professor Lubimov states that

Lomonosov's theories on electricity and air are sounder than all

the contemporary theories on the subject. The most important of

all his theories on physics is his rejection of the hypothesis of

heat elements and his own theory that heat is motion of a special

type. It would be desirable for modern scientists to give a critical

estimate of Lomonosov's work in the field of natural science, al-

though it is manifest that he was a naturalist of extraordinary

ability. "All the notes of Lomonosov in the field of physics and

chemistry are not only good but excellent," wrote his contemporary,

the famous Haller, "because he clearly and basically explains the

most curious phenomena that have remained inexplicable to our great-

est geniuses, and I am fully convinced of the correctness of his

interpretations."

The question of Lomonosov's merit as a naturalist should

be studied by Russian historians of natural sciences. The future

that befell the scientific works of Lomonosov is shrouded in mystery.

An inquiry into this fate is even more important for the history
of Russian social thought, as well as the history of the Europeanization of Russia, than a study of his scientific achievements as
such. Bulich was the first who asked this question:

> Why did not contemporary European science take advantage of
> his ingenious discoveries? Why did not Russian scholars who
> worked along the same lines pay any attention to his work,
> the work that would give them a sound understanding of science
> and liberate them from the necessity of repeating European
> errors?[1]

"A prophet hath no honor in his own country," nor among
his own kin - that is the answer. In Russia we recognize the talents
of our authors only after the West has bowed to them. I do not
argue the merits or demerits of such an attitude. The reasons are
to be found in the sociopsychological conditions of the Russian
people. Lomonosov was the first Russian who was not appreciated
either at home or abroad, although he well deserved it. Indeed,
others have fared just as badly. Geniuses and books have a peculiar
fate which is determined by the part played by their own country
in the development of civilization.

Although Lomonosov's work in the field of natural science
is exceptional, he did not accomplish all that he might have done.
Circumstances in his life made him dissipate his ability. I have
only to mention the many laudatory speeches which he was commanded

---

1

The essay "M. V. Lomonosov" by N. V. Bulich in X. A. Vengerov,
<u>Russian Poetry</u>, St. Petersburg, 1893, p. 94.

to compose. This took up much of his time. His other writings, although of a more serious character, made further inroads on his work capacity and distracted him from the subject dearest to his heart - natural science. Besides, he devoted himself to educational pursuits. "My only wish is to bring our university to the point where it can produce an unlimited number of Lomonosovs," he once wrote to Shuvalov.

We know how persistently he pleaded for the opening of the University of Moscow and what he did for its development. A short time later, Lomonosov tried to reconstruct the University of St. Petersburg. He desired to see it function independently of the Academy of Science. His dreams were not realized until the time of Alexander I. Textbooks and manuals were necessary for these educational institutions. Lomonosov undertook their preparation. He wrote A Short Textbook on Rhetoric, A Short Textbook for the Orator, Russian Grammar, Can Churchbooks Benefit the Russian Language?[1] These are not all of his activities as an enlightener,

---

[1] In the dedication of his Russian Grammar, Lomonosov wrote: "The Roman Emperor, Charles V, used to say that one should speak Spanish in addressing God, French in talking with friends, German in dealing with enemies and Italian when conversing with a woman. But had he known Russian, he would, no doubt, have added that one could talk to any and all of them in Russian. He would have found in Russian the grandeur of Spanish, the grace of French, the strength of German, the tenderness of Italian, besides the wealth and conciseness of Greek and Latin. I am certain of this because I have been using Russian for a long time. The powerful eloquence of Cicero, the epic grandeur of Vergil, the charming poetry of Ovid do not lose their flavor when translated into Russian. Philosophic thoughts can be expressed in our language just as precisely as in any other; we have a corresponding terminology to describe phenomena with which the natural sciences deal. And if there is something we cannot express, it is not because of the poverty of our language, but because of the lack in our knowledge." (Works, vol. 4, p. 10.)

but clearly, to accomplish even this much, one needed time; time
which he could otherwise have devoted to natural science. The
educator in Lomonosov was fighting the scholar in him, and prevented him from developing to the fullest extent his extraordinary
scientific abilities. Lomonosov, however, could not refuse to
work for the cause of education; his love of Russia did not permit
it.

Our enlighteners were always most active in the field
of social thought. Some of them were great theorists, but their
work as educators always took them away from science. They themselves recognized this only too well. Chernyshevsky, occupying a
place of distinction among the enlighteners, expressed this opinion:

> Many great German, French and English educators have no direct
> contact with the welfare of their country; many great scientists
> poets, and artists serve "art for art's sake" and not for the
> "welfare of their Fatherland." This is impossible in our
> country. In time we will have thinkers and artists who will
> work only in the interest of science and art; but until we be-
> come the cultural equals of the progressive nations, all of
> us cherish another task more: to help develop, as much as we
> can, what Peter the Great started. This has been necessary
> until now, and it will probably continue to be so for some
> time to come. All rational and moral forces of our Fatherland
> are needed for the accomplishment of one foremost task.

Thus is explained much of the fate not only of Lomonosov
but of our other enlighteners as well.[1]

---

[1]
N. Chernyshevsky, "Sketches on the Gogol Period of Russian Literature," Works, St. Petersburg, 1906, vol. 2, pp. 120-122.